TEXTILE & PATTERN DESIGN: WIENER WERKSTÄTTE TO AMERICAN MO

JACQUELINE GROA

Geoffrey Rayner
Richard Chamberlain
Annamarie Stapleton

Antique Collectors' Club

For H. Kirk Brown III and Jill A. Wiltse,
without whose friendship, enthusiasm and support
this book would not have been possible

©2009 Geoffrey Rayner, Richard Chamberlain, Annamarie Stapleton

First published 2009
Reprinted 2015

World copyright reserved

ISBN 978-1-85149-590-0

The right of Geoffrey Rayner, Richard Chamberlain and Annamarie Stapleton to be identified as authors of this work has been asserted by them in accordance with the Copyright, Designs and Patents Act 1988

British Library Cataloguing-in-Publication Data

A catalogue record for this book is available from the British Library

Printed in China for the Antique Collectors' Club Ltd, Woodbridge, Suffolk

Cover image Roller-printed textile, 1952 by Jacqueline Groag for David Whitehead Ltd. Photograph by Steve Tanner

MIX
Paper from
responsible sources
FSC
www.fsc.org **FSC® C021256**

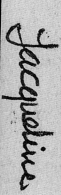

CONTENTS

Acknowledgements

Sadly, Karin Williger died soon after correcting the final draft of her account and we are grateful to her son, Zac Manasseh, for allowing us to use it and to other members of her family and friends who generously helped with additional information and family anecdotes. Numerous other people have been generous with their contributions of time, knowledge and images and in particular we would like to thank: Isabelle Anscombe; Angela Brill; H Kirk Brown III & Jill A Wiltse-Brown; Michelle Brown at the London Transport Museum; Anna Buruma and the Liberty Archive; Trevor and Elaine Chamberlain; Alan Cook and the Cummersdale Design Collection; Mark Eastment; Judy Faraday and Linda Moroney at the John Lewis Partnership Archive Collection; Francesca Galloway; the Groag Family; Clifford Hatts; Lesley Hoskins; Alan and Kate Irvine; Lesley Jackson; Wilhelm and Janet Kaulbach; Catherine Moriarty and the Design Council Archive, University of Brighton; David Morris; James Mosse; Alison Musker; the National Art Library; Graham Pointer; Ursula Prokop: Sue Riley; Pat Schleger; Shanna Shelby; Steve Tanner; Margaret Timmers; Margarete Titz at the Böhlau Verlag Wien; the Victoria & Albert Museum Department of Prints and Drawings and the Victoria & Albert Museum Archive of Art and Design; Angela Völker; Eva White at the Archive of Art and Design. Our thanks, also, to James Smith and Prim Elliott at ACC for commissioning and editing the book and Orna Frommer-Dawson and Geoff Windram for their design. Last, but not least, to family and friends who have supported us during this project: thank you.

ACKNOWLEDGEMENTS

I first met Jacqueline Groag in 1981 in her small ground-floor flat in Ovington Square, near Harrods, when I was writing *A Woman's Touch* (Virago, 1984). The interior was soft and sophisticated, furnished with interesting creamy textures and small paintings. Nearing eighty, she had recently completed a self-portrait, which she showed me. In light pastel colours – I recall yellow and white – it was the perfect invocation of the woman I went to talk to: an enterprising professional designer who, with her husband, had had to leave Austria and establish herself all over again in a new country; a widow; a twentieth century woman with strong views about feminism, marriage, work, money, domestic duties, children, contemporary design. Her self-portrait depicted an eight-year-old girl who was nevertheless also that woman.

Jacqueline – I can still hear her announcing herself on the 'phone, pronouncing her name in softened consonants – had trained in Vienna under Franz Cizek, who encouraged his students never to lose their connection with the spontaneous visual expression they had exercised as children. She also explained her theory that everyone is, all their lives, a particular age. She was eight. And, looking at her work, which, in the clarity of its line and colour as much as subject-matter, eluded received notions and never lost an element of childlike wonder, of day-dreaming, I thought she was right.

She seemed a little lonely – or just hungry for new people and impressions – and somewhat frightened of old age, and I visited her several times. She was outward-looking, courageous, generous, held clear opinions gently expressed, and laughed often: it was wonderful to know her. When my daughter was born, she gave me a small, brightly-coloured drawing of four young girls, and I am always amazed when people ask if it was my daughter who painted it, as no child could possibly have used such technique or conveyed such a sophisticated directness of vision. But I suspect she would have enjoyed their misapprehension.

Isabelle Anscombe

AN APPRECIATION

Jacqueline Groag 1950s.
Private collection

[1] Lesley Jackson, *20th Century Pattern Design: Textile and Wallpaper Pioneers,* Mitchell Beazley, London, 2002, p.6.

[2] A. Sarnitz, *Loos,* Taschen, Cologne, 2003 pp.84-89. Loos' 1908 essay, first published in English in 1913, reprinted in Sarnitz's 2003 publication.

[3] M. Pachmanova, Conference paper, 'Civilized Woman: Czech Functionalism and the Cultivation of Femininity', Design History Society/Norwich School of Art and Design Conference, 2003.

[4] Le Corbusier, *Towards a New Architecture,* trans. Frederick Etchells, Rodker, London 1927.

[5] Christopher Reed, Conference paper, 'Designs for (Queer) Living; Amusing Design of the 1920s (Bloomsbury Design)', Design History Society/Norwich School of Art and Design Conference, 2003.

[6] Le Corbusier.

[7] Ursula Prokop, *Das Architekten und Designer – Ehepaar, Jacques und Jacqueline Groag, Zwei vergessene Kunstler der Wiener Moderne,* Bohlau Verlag, Wien, Köln, Weimar, 2005, p.55.

[8] Angela Volker, *Textiles of the Wiener Werkstätte 1910-1932,* Thames & Hudson, London, 1994, p.116.

[9] Christopher Reed, *Bloomsbury Rooms, Modernism, Subculture, and Domesticity,* published for The Bard Graduate Center for Studies in the Decorative Arts, Design and Culture, New York, by Yale University Press, New Haven and London, 2004.

[10] Benno Reifenberg, 'West – Kunst – Gewerbe, Zur internationalen Ausstellung in Paris', *Frankfurter Zeitung,* 5 August 1925.

Jacqueline Groag was one of the small group of talented pioneer women designers who were influential in the development of Modernist design and culture in early twentieth century Europe. Many were designers of major significance – albeit from rival schools of modernity – such as France's Charlotte Perriand, Ireland's Eileen Gray and Germany's Marianne Brandt and a number who, like Jacqueline, remain less well known. Few received recognition of their achievements in their lifetimes, or at least not until comparatively late in their careers – careers that were, in the main, overshadowed by those of their male counterparts. Jacqueline's chosen path, that of pattern design, only further served to obscure the brilliance of her international achievement, particularly in the field of textile design. Lesley Jackson, in her book *20th Century Pattern Design: Textile and Wallpaper Pioneers,* comments that:

Given the obvious appeal of textiles and wallpapers, it has always surprised me that surface pattern has so often been marginalized within mainstream histories of 20th-century design. While the achievements of William Morris during the 19th century are widely recognised, very few pattern designers since then have been awarded the same degree of attention.[1]

A great deal of this marginalization, and subsequent neglect and trivialisation of pattern design and decoration, has its origins in the early twentieth century when, despite a wide spectrum of schools of modernity, design and architectural theory was increasingly dominated by the rational, reductive and functionalist concepts of male architects such as Adolf Loos, Le Corbusier and Mies van der Rohe. Their influence and authority continued to grow until the 1930s and the apotheosis of the style of the International Modern Movement associated with the Bauhaus and Le Corbusier.

Up to this point there were still a number of particularly distinctive voices in the general cacophony of competing versions of Modernity. However, it was the sparse minimalism of Bauhausian-influenced design and architecture that was increasingly hailed, within mainstream western European Modernist culture, as the ultimate achievement. Opposed to this purity was the perceived decadence of a more decorative modernity, such as that associated with the Vienna Secession, particularly the avant-garde domesticity of the later work of Josef Hoffmann and the Wiener Werkstätte, or the decorative expressionism of the

Amsterdam School in Holland and, in Britain, the sub-cultural Feminine or Gay post-Impressionist aesthetic of Bloomsbury and the Omega Workshops.

Although each of these were valid interpretations of twentieth century modernity, amongst the influential doyens of the International Modern Movement surface pattern and decoration were dismissed as superficial and unimportant. In Adolf Loos' polemical pamphlet of 1908, 'Ornament and Crime', he equates decoration with what he sees as the primitive and criminal activities of graffiti and tattooing. For Loos, decoration and ornamentation equalled degeneration which he directly connected with women and savages and the reverse, a lack of decoration, as the pinnacle of human achievement and conversely the removal of ornament as cultural evolution.[2] Of Modernist attitudes to 'Femininity' in 1920s Czechoslovakia, M. Pachmanova writes that,

Czech modernist architects and designers were quick to adopt Loosian ideals, and especially in the 1920s and the beginning of the 1930s declared war not only on ornament, but also on all socio-cultural phenomena that did not conform to assumed signs of progress, including Femininity.[3]

In 1925, in *Towards a New Architecture*, Le Corbusier writes of his domestic ideal of the house as 'a machine for living in', in opposition to the traditional 'cult of the home' with 'rooms too small, a conglomeration of useless and disparate objects ... and absurd bric-a-brac'.[4] Christopher Reed views Le Corbusier's house as 'a corrective version of Modernism' in which the 'properly masculine engineers aesthetic suppressed design styles'[5] that Le Corbusier compared to 'unclean orchids, ... blue hortensias and green chrysanthemums'.[6] Such attitudes were as dismissive of the textiles of the artists Raoul Dufy and Sonia Delaunay, and products in the French inspired Art Deco style, as those of the avant-garde Wiener Werkstätte.

Ursula Prokop has noted that in Austria in the early part of the twentieth century an education in the applied arts was practically the only artistic option available to women as virtually all fine art academies refused to accept them.[7] It is perhaps no surprise then that in the years immediately following the end of the First World War an increasing number of the Wiener Werkstätte designers were women, most of whom were former students of Josef Hoffmann from the Wien Kunstgewerbeschule (Vienna Arts and Craft School). It was from then on that women had 'a virtual monopoly in determining how the Wiener Werkstätte and its products would be viewed'.[8]

Whilst they designed a wide variety of avant-garde domestic objects, both functional and decorative, many of their designs for the Werkstätte from the 1920s were for furnishing and fashion textiles. By that time avant-garde pattern design and the decorative arts in general were caricatured by their misogynistic and patronizing opponents as 'feminine' occupations: superficial and insignificant, something for women and dilettantes to indulge in. Christopher Reed, writing on this subject with reference to Bloomsbury and the Omega Workshops, comments on 'the usual priorities of art history which have made the notion of avant-garde domesticity an oxymoron, in the process removing Bloomsbury's paintings from the canon of modernism and refusing to consider the murals, ceramics, textiles, and wallpapers as art at all'.[9]

Following the Werkstätte's showing at the 1925 Paris Exposition Internationale, Adolf Loos' diatribes against its products became increasingly fierce and vehement. Benno Reifenberg, echoing Le Corbusier, wrote of the displays that 'the Wiener Werkstätte has poured its trifling life into these showcases, the bric-a-brac of the boudoir, fashion and toys; a motley pile out of Santa Claus's sack'.[10]

As a former Arts and Crafts student of Hoffmann's at the Kunstgewerbeschule, and a female designer of textiles for the Wiener Werkstätte, Jacqueline Groag would have been a prime candidate for the disapprobation of the devotees of the International Modern Movement. However, in her case there were also other, more sinister, forces at work. It was from amongst the highly educated and cultured Jewish middle classes that many of the patrons of, and leading contributors to, Vienna's dazzling intellectual and artistic life in the early twentieth century were drawn, and Jacqueline, like many of the women of the Werkstätte, was Jewish. In Austria in the early twentieth century there was a heavy undercurrent of anti-Semitism. This became particularly clear during the rise of National Socialism, when the Werkstätte became the target of numerous defamatory articles.

Given all of this, it is hardly surprising that the remarkable achievements of the creators of surface design in the early twentieth century, particularly avant-garde textile designers – who were mainly women – should have been obscured and marginalised, and their contribution to the enhancement of the quality and pleasure of people's daily lives trivialised. This dismissive attitude towards the art of pattern design and decoration had a long afterlife, which continued amongst Modernist architects and designers until recent times and the advent of Post Modernism.

Post Second World War, the defeat of Fascism and the retreat of authoritarian and totalitarian attitudes created an environment in which art movements such as Surrealism, Abstract Expressionism and the increasing influence of popular culture were able to contribute to a more relaxed and inclusive attitude to pattern and decoration. Following the trauma of the war, with its tight controls and general deprivation and limitations, there was a reaction against the narrow dictates of functionalist design and an eagerness to indulge in colour and pattern that continued into the 1970s.

Jacqueline was extremely well placed to take a leading role in this remarkable post-war renaissance of pattern design, particularly that of textiles. Fortunately, she and her husband, the Modernist architect Jacques Groag, fleeing the Nazis in 1939, chose to settle in London. Although the anglophile Loos had praised what he saw as the restrained elegance and functionalist qualities of British design, the British were never entirely at ease with the standardised mass-produced functional products and reductive style associated with the ideals of the International Modern Movement. They had always had a penchant for the graphic and decorative arts, particularly two-dimensional linear design and, since the late eighteenth century, had led the world in the manufacture of textiles, especially printed cottons.

On her arrival in Britain Jacqueline found herself in a sympathetic environment with support and semi-official backing from influential individuals such as Gordon Russell and Charles Reilly, both later knighted for their contributions to architecture and design. In fact, large numbers of intellectual and artistic émigrés from Eastern Europe were actively encouraged and embraced with the British Government's open support.[11] The perilous state of the British economy in the early 1940s meant exports, particularly those for the overseas textile market, were an important financial contributor to the war effort as well as a useful form of propaganda. It was recognized there was a need to improve the standard of design for the export market and Jacqueline, with an established international reputation, was welcomed as an important asset. Throughout the 1940s she was a leading designer of both furnishing and fashion textiles in Britain, and her translation and development of her earlier work – particularly that for the Werkstätte –

combined with her remarkable originality, largely set the standard for the 1950s.

In the years between 1937 and 1946, Jacqueline's path and that of Karin Williger, a younger Jewish woman from Vienna, ran parallel, occasionally crossing and re-crossing, until eventually they intertwined for a few years. Karin was the only assistant Jacqueline is known to have employed. Her first-hand account of those extraordinary years conveys something of the dramatic circumstances of the time, and the ever-present sense of fear and danger that people in their position learnt to live and work with, and eventually overcome.

Opposite Karin Williger photographed by Robert Haas in Vienna 1938. Courtesy of Zac Manasseh

[11] Andrew Marr, *A History of Modern Britain*, Macmillan, 2007.

Karin's Story

I trained as a textile designer whilst working in England as Jacqueline Groag's assistant during the Second World War. Prior to this, my association with Jacqueline's circle went back many years to pre-war Vienna. I come from an assimilated Austrian Jewish family who, like many others, had converted to Christianity. They were intellectual and cultured people: my uncle – my mother's brother – Professor Hans Kelsen, one of the twentieth century's leading international jurists, had written the constitution of the first Austrian republic, and my parents, Richard and Gertrude Weiss, were generous and enlightened patrons of the arts, especially of newly emerging young sculptors and architects.

My first encounter with the Groags was in 1937, when my parents commissioned Jacqueline's husband, Jacques, to design

a combined studio-bedsitting room for me. Jacques was a gentle and sensitive man, whom both my mother and I very much admired. He was a well-known Modernist architect and had trained and worked in Vienna with the legendary Adolf Loos, originator of the well-known slogan 'ornament is crime'. This sentiment did not always hold true for his students though, for the cushions of the sofa-bed Jacques had designed for me were covered with a floral textile designed by Jacqueline. Another architect from that time, whom my family knew well and whose work we respected, was the handsome young Hungarian architect Stefan Buzas. A good friend of the Groags, Stefan was to play an influential role in Jacqueline's and my lives much later in England.

I was eighteen when Jacques designed the studio-bedsitting room for me, and that September I joined the preliminary course at the Wien Kunstgewerbeschule, then under the direction of Professor Josef Hoffmann. He was a

revered Secessionist architect, designer and founder of the Wiener Werkstätte. I had attended the school for only two terms when, in March 1938, the political union of Germany and Austria, the *Anschluss,* was declared and the German army entered Vienna. When I returned, at the beginning of the summer term, to the Kunstgewerbeschule, members of the Nazi special police force, the Schutzstaffel or SS, were standing at the entrance. All non-Aryans were refused admission, and my brief time at the Schule came to an abrupt end.

Until then I had never had any personal contact with Hoffmann, so I was extremely surprised when, quite out of the blue, I received a telephone call from him, asking me, without any explanation, to urgently meet him that afternoon in the Belvedere, a park near my home. I was so in awe of him I accepted his strange invitation without question. Upon meeting we sat on a bench and, to my amazement, he grasped my hand and made me swear never to reveal to anyone my liaison with him. Astounded by this bizarre request, I promised faithfully to carry it out, whereupon he quickly and furtively departed, and I neither saw nor heard anything of him again.

He had a certain reputation amongst the students and was probably concerned that any affairs he may have had with Jewish students should not come to the attention of the SS, as a sexual relationship between an Aryan and non-Aryan – *Rassenschande* (racial disgrace) – was a serious criminal offence under the Nazi apartheid. My only explanation for this odd encounter is that in his anxiety to cover his tracks he was asking the same thing of all the Jewish girls who had recently studied at the Kunstgewerbeschule. I was probably a case of mistaken identity or, perhaps even, confused anticipation! Both my brothers left Austria soon after this but, before leaving, my elder brother Thomas, in order to get me a British passport, arranged a marriage of convenience for me with a British theatrical producer, Herbert Williger.

At that time I was already romantically involved with the Modernist photographer, Robert Haas, a pupil and former assistant of Trude Fleischmann, the distinguished Viennese photographer. I had become Robert's studio assistant and it was not long after that I was mistaken by the SS for an Aryan and arrested for being in a sexual relationship with a Jew.

The SS held me in Robert's studio until he returned. I tried to shout to warn him but they threatened me at gunpoint, saying they would shoot if I did not keep quiet. When they discovered I was a Jewish convert to Christianity and the charge did not stand, we were released. Having drawn so much adverse attention to ourselves, Robert left pretty quickly for England and I joined him a little later, after keeping a low profile in the countryside outside Vienna.

Early in 1939 the Viennese émigré architect and designer Franz Singer commissioned a large photomontage from Robert for the restaurant of the new John Lewis department store in London's Oxford Street. The mural, with my assistance, of course, was a great success, but life in England was not quite as Robert had hoped and that summer he left for the United States. I followed soon after, having first tempted fate by returning to Vienna to obtain the fare from my parents. Somewhat ironically, because I now held a British passport I could neither claim refugee status nor obtain a green card in the US and I had to return to England. Once back I worked for a time with my brother Thomas at the Camphill-Rudolf Steiner School in Scotland. However, my priority was to obtain a divorce from Herbert Williger and to accomplish this I needed to return to London. On arriving in London I was directed, as a form of war work, to employment as an assistant in a kindergarten in

Hampstead. I became very depressed and it was my old friend from Vienna, Stefan Buzas, who, as always, came to my rescue.

Stefan had also come to England just before the war and was a central figure in the London-based group of Viennese émigrés of which I was part. The Groags, who had arrived in London in August 1939, were also great friends of Stefan's, and he insisted I accompany him to dinner at their apartment in the fashionable

Isokon Lawn Road flats. Hence I renewed my acquaintance with Jacques and Jacqueline. Their apartment was small, but immaculate in shades of white and beautifully, if sparsely, furnished in the severe architectural style of the Bauhaus, with each object carefully placed as in a stage set. Jacqueline was equally imposing. Delicate and petite, she was somewhat exotic, almost, I felt, oriental in appearance and immaculately dressed in white or very pale colours. I particularly remember a pair of wide culotte trousers she often wore, made in a finely pleated white material, which elegantly split open over her feet. Everything about Jacqueline, from her home, to her appearance and her work, was always intensely thought through. Shortly after this Jacqueline approached me, I am sure at Stefan's behest, to ask if I would like to become her assistant. Of course I accepted. I was full of admiration for her and Jacques' work and here was an opportunity, in some way, to recommence my studies after their being forcibly broken off in 1938.

The apartment in Albany Terrace, near Regent's Park, in which Jacqueline had her studio, had a bathroom and kitchen, as well as two smaller rooms, one of which served me both as a bedsitting room and a studio. Jacqueline taught me the technicalities of textile design, my principal task as her assistant being to put her designs into repeats and to devise colourways. Living and working surrounded by Jacqueline's designs was a constant source of inspiration for me. Her work in Vienna and Paris before the Second World War had given Jacqueline a distinguished international reputation which placed her in a privileged position when she arrived in Britain. Due to government restrictions very few well-coloured and patterned textiles were produced during the war, other than those intended for the export market, many of which Jacqueline designed. Buyers from the northern textile manufacturers would regularly visit 'Madame' Groag, as she was then known, to purchase designs, and she would often give them a bed for the night in the spare room, enabling them to save their board and lodging allowances. My part in this arrangement was to provide breakfast and collect their morning newspapers. Some of these buyers, having seen my work, also bought my designs which was a great encouragement for me. Jacqueline was not happy about this and she moved not long after, a situation that caused me considerable sadness then, and can still do so now.

Following Jacqueline's departure I continued to live and work in the apartment

at Albany Terrace which I shared with
a girlfriend, Susan Cox. Susan was the wife
of the distinguished architect Anthony (later
Sir Anthony) Cox, then serving in the army
in India. Working from Jacqueline's former
studio I successfully established myself as an
independent textile designer and, despite
my fears, did not starve. I designed some well-
received textiles for Alastair Morton and
Edinburgh Weavers, for Gerald Holtom and
the John Lewis Partnership, some of which were
published in the *Studio Year Book of Decorative
Art* and *The Ambassador*. I later felt particularly
honoured when, in 1955, Michael Farr, in his
influential work *Design in British Industry*,
illustrated one of my textiles which he described
'as characteristic of the most gifted textile
designers'. Yet, after my hectic lifestyle of the
previous ten years, I was happy enough to
exchange my career for a home and children
when I married my second husband, the architect
Leonard Manasseh, in 1947.

Jacqueline Groag, who was such an inspiration to me in my youth, was a
visionary, an extraordinarily intense, brilliant, original and dedicated
individual for whom art, design and personal life were one and the same,
almost a spiritual unity, and someone from whom I learnt a great deal which
remains with me still. *Karin Williger, April 2008*

Opposite Karin Williger
photographed by Robert
Haas at St Goddard's College,
Plainfield, Vermont, USA,
in 1939. Haas, with whom
Karin had been romantically
involved in Vienna, was
teaching calligraphy and
photography at the college
at that time. Courtesy of Zac
Manasseh

Left *Galante* screen-printed
textured cotton, designed by
Karin Williger, circa 1946, and
produced by Edinburgh
Weavers in 1949. Collection
H. Kirk Brown III and
Jill A. Wiltse

Left Pen and ink drawing by Karin Williger of Susan Cox at Albany Terrace, circa 1946. Courtesy of Joanna Cox

Right *Borrogrove* screen-printed textured cotton designed by Karin Williger, and produced by Edinburgh Weavers in 1949. Collection H. Kirk Brown III and Jill A. Wiltse

In the years following the end of the Second World War, the textile and pattern designer Jacqueline Groag, a disciple and pupil of Josef Hoffmann and a survivor from the sophisticated and cultured world of early twentieth century Vienna, introduced to Britain and the United States the tolerant, inclusive and decorative modernity associated with the Wien Kunstgewerbeschule and the Wiener Werkstätte, a modernity previously found

wanting and dismissed by the doyens of the International Modern Movement. For some twenty years she had a leading part in the renaissance of pattern design which occurred in the aftermath of the war, when people had a strong desire for decoration and colour in their homes and daily lives: a desire that continued throughout the 1950s and 1960s. Although largely a reaction against the strictures of the war, it was also a rejection of the functionalist and somewhat authoritarian precepts of pre-war International Modernism. Despite the missionary activities in the post-war period of the principal propagandists of rational design – in Britain the Council of Industrial Design and in the United States New York's Museum of Modern Art – popular demand for pattern and decoration proved irrepressible.

Ironically, it was the war that laid the foundations of the growing prosperity enjoyed by the majority of people in the late 1940s and 1950s. Both the war effort and post-war reconstruction brought about full employment, and the new technologies and scientific advances created in the forcing house of wartime needs helped fuel the economic recovery. The general mood was increasingly optimistic and celebratory and there was a determination that neither the economic depression of the pre-war era nor the trauma of the war should ever happen again. The brave new world envisaged for the future was epitomised by the new towns built in Britain in the late 1940s and early 1950s by the radical post-war Labour government, and in the U.S.A. by the houses built by Levitt and Sons. The inexpensive 'dream houses' of the Levittowns came to typify 1950s American suburbia.

With increasing confidence in the growing contents of their wage packets and easy access to credit through hire purchase agreements, most people concentrated the fruits of their new affluence on their homes. Jonathan Woodham writes that:

Above Jacqueline Groag, published in *The Ambassador*, 1956.

Opposite The Secession building, Vienna, Austria, designed by J.M. Olbrich, 1897-8.

12 Jonathan M. Woodham, *Twentieth-century Ornament,* Rizzoli International Publications Inc, New York, 1990, p.194.

13 Isabelle Anscombe, taped interview with Jacqueline Groag, 1981. Anscombe Archive, Newnham College, Cambridge.

14 Ibid.

15 Ibid.

16 Isabelle Anscombe, conversation with the authors, August 2008.

...extra attention was paid to the embellishment of the domestic environment which now became a priority. The widely encouraged use of ornament and decoration was characteristic of the late 1940s and 1950s; and all manner of contemporary motifs were employed, often combined with the latest technology to indulge the whims of a public eager to display its material wealth.[12]

The new television sets, radiograms, three piece suites and cocktail bars were set against backgrounds of patterned textiles, wallpapers and brightly coloured paint. Following the riot of decoration and colour associated with the Festival of Britain in 1951, such lively and vivid interiors were also to be seen in many new public and commercial spaces. Much of the 'Contemporary' style of the textiles and wallpapers shown at the Festival was heavily indebted to Jacqueline Groag's work in the 1940s. By 1951, already with a distinguished career of some twenty-five years, Jacqueline was a leading designer of textiles and her work a major influence on pattern design internationally.

1903-1929: Early Years
The Wien Kunstgewerbeschule
and the Wiener Werkstätte

Although Viennese in attitude and culture, Jacqueline and her husband, Jacques, were originally Czech, subjects of the Hapsburg Emperors of the former Austro-Hungarian Empire. Jacqueline was born Hilde Pick in Prague in 1903. She was a member of an assimilated middle class Jewish family, but had abandoned the religion of her ancestors and, unlike Jacques, who although not especially religious never forsook his Jewishness, was without any faith until she later became a devout Roman Catholic. When interviewed in 1981,[13] her attitude towards her father, an industrialist who died in the First World War, seemed somewhat ambiguous. She appeared much closer to her mother, whose family she described with warmth and enthusiasm as extremely creative, many of whom, she said, were artists, writers, poets and printmakers.[14]

As a child she had been extremely delicate and in poor health and, unlike her siblings, was educated at home. Although she studied all the usual subjects of the *lycée* she never took any formal exams, which she felt had, together with her relative isolation from other children and the outside world, left her a 'sophisticated naïf'.[15] It was to this perceived naivety that she attributed the charm, apparent artlessness and simplicity of her artistic vision. She later developed a theory that, besides their chronological age, everyone is born with an inner age which remains constant throughout their life and determines what and who they are. Importantly, for her future career, Jacqueline felt her inner age to be eight.[16]

Following the collapse of the Hapsburg Empire at the end of the First World War, its constituent nations became independent states, but Vienna, the old imperial capital, with its sophisticated intellectual and artistic life, remained the cultural lodestone for many of the empire's former subjects. Jacqueline, widowed at the age of twenty after a short marriage to a Herr Blumberger, decided, like many others, to seek her fortune in Vienna. The brilliant cultural life of the city in the 1920s partly had its origins in the late 1890s with the founding of the Vienna Secession, one of the first, if not the first, proto-modernist movements in Europe. Although originally a group of young painters led by Gustav Klimt who seceded in 1897 from the constraints and reactionary policies of the central bastion of the Viennese art establishment, the Künstlerhaus, the Secession also included amongst its members architects and designers such as Otto Wagner, Josef Hoffmann and Joseph Maria Olbrich.

The aim of many radical young architects and designers of the time was the Gesamtkunstwerk, a synthesis of architecture and the fine and applied arts in a total work of art. In an attempt to achieve this, two leading members of the Secession, the architect Josef Hoffmann and the designer Koloman Moser, backed financially by the industrialist Fritz Warndorfer, founded the Wiener Werkstätte in 1903. The Werkstätte was originally conceived as an association of artist-craftsmen, set up for the production of high quality modern furnishings and decorative art, designed by architects and designers connected with the Secession. By 1910 the Werkstätte had lost much of its idealism and was becoming, from financial necessity, increasingly commercialised. Moser and fellow

Top right Cushion cover
designed by Jacqueline Groag
for the Wiener Werkstätte,
circa 1929.

Bottom right Design for
wallpaper exhibited at
Suffolk Galleries' exhibition,
1945, based on a design
Jacqueline had executed in
1929 whilst still in Vienna,
studying under Hoffman.

Opposite *Adler,* a printed
cotton designed by Josef
Hoffmann, circa 1910.
Private Collection

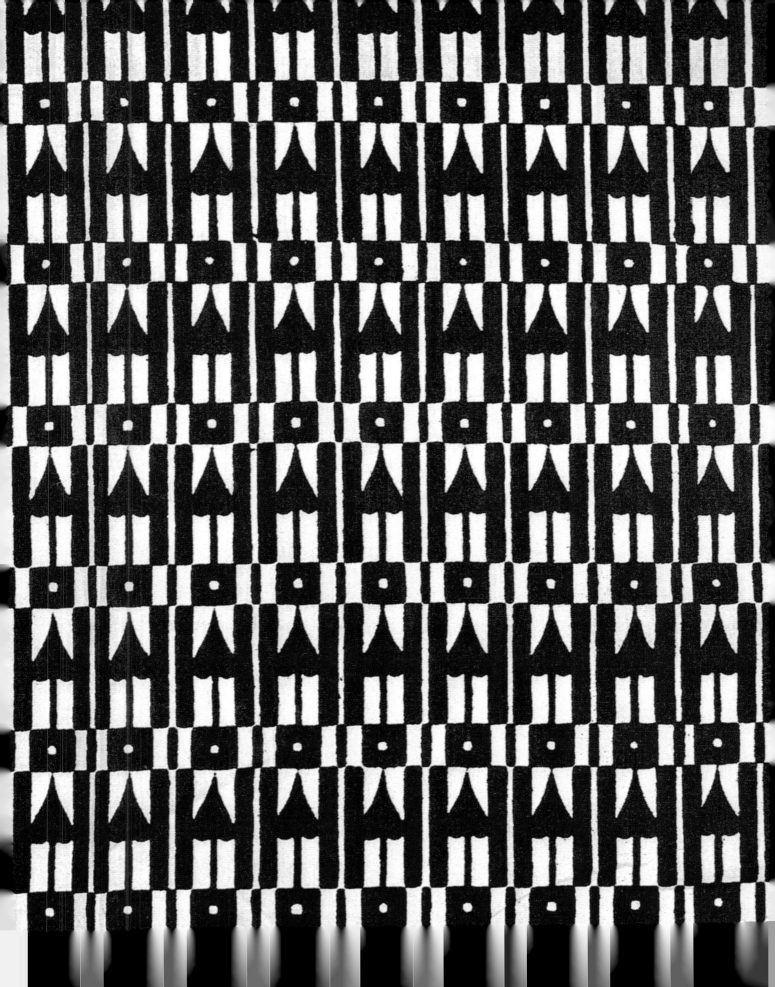

Above Pediment (detail), a design from Bond Worth's Acropolis range of carpets, 1957. This design is an outstanding example of Jacqueline's continuing use of the Wiener Werkstätte style of some fifty years earlier.

[17] Christopher Reed, *Bloomsbury Rooms, Modernism, Subculture and Domesticity*, published for The Bard Graduate Center for Studies in the Decorative Arts, Design and Culture, New York, by Yale University Press, New Haven and London, 2004, p.5.

[18] Ibid.

[19] Anscombe/Groag.

[20] Ibid.

[21] Ibid.

[22] Prokop, 'Die Bekanntschaft mit Hilde Blumberger', pp.55-59.

[23] Hans Von Ankwicz, 'Arbeiten von Hilde Blumberger-Wien', *Deutsche Kunst und Dekoration*, 1930, Vol. XXXIII, p.125.

[24] Margaret Timmers, interview with the authors, May 2008.

[25] Ankwicz.

[26] Anscombe/Groag.

[27] Jacques & Jacqueline Groag Archive, handwritten note in the Archive of Art & Design, Victoria and Albert Museum, London (AAD).

[28] Anscombe/Groag.

[29] Prokop. p.111.

[30] Ibid.

[31] Timmers.

designer Carl Otto Czeschka had left and much more eclectic and ornamental styles were replacing the more severe geometry associated with the early Werkstätte. Although remaining under Hoffmann's direction until its closure in 1932, the influence of Eduard Wimmer-Wisgrill and Dagobert Peche began to dominate the Werkstätte's decorative style and the opening of the fashion and textile departments in 1910 and 1911 was considered by many a dilution of its original aims.

From early on many of the designers in the textile department were former students of Hoffmann's from the Kunstgewerbeschule; most were women, many were Jewish. This became increasingly so after the end of the First World War. In the 1920s the Werkstätte was remarkable for the influence of women designers on its style and products, evolving in the process an 'avant-garde domesticity'[17] which, with the addition of fashion, created an essentially 'Feminine' interpretation of Modernity.[18] It was to this sophisticated milieu surrounding the Werkstätte that Jacqueline gained admission when she became a student at the Kunstgewerbeschule. Following the death of her first husband it was an imperative for her to establish her independence and decorative art and design provided one of the few areas in which women could forge a professional career.

Her first academic year at the Kunstgewerbeschule, 1926-27, was spent studying 'General Study of Form' on the preliminary course with the well-known progressive teacher of art and design, Professor Franz Cizek. He had developed an unorthodox method of teaching art and design based on children's art, in which he encouraged his students to forget any formal art training they had previously received and to develop anew a child's naive and innocent vision of the world.

Jacqueline, of course, was received with open arms by Cizek, who was delighted with her lack of any formal art training, and she soon became a star pupil, making rapid progress under his teaching methods.[19]

She later recalled, with great pleasure, how in the afternoons Cizek would often hand out ten different coloured chalks and an identical small drawing pad to each student and set them a drawing project. Music was always played during the class for the students to lose themselves in and to be inspired by. The resulting work was then placed on the studio walls and Cizek would hold a group critique.[20] Jacqueline thrived so much under Cizek's teaching that he arranged with Hoffmann for both her end of year exams and the entrance requirements for admission to the Kunstgewerbeschule's design course to be waived. It was also at Cizek's suggestion that she chose to study pattern design and she spent her remaining two years at the Kunstgewerbeschule in Hoffmann's architecture classes, where she specialised in the design of textiles, wallpapers, carpets and posters.[21]

Her exceptional ability and talent was recognised when she won first prize in a competition, organised by the Kunstgewerbeschule, for the design of a poster to promote the Salzburg Festival that year. She was also awarded first prize in a competition for a textile design for the Wiener Werkstätte.[22] While she was still a student many of her textile designs were bought by the Werkstätte and after leaving college she continued to sell work to them on a freelance basis. The influence of Hoffmann's teaching was to remain with her for the rest of her life and she continued to develop and spread the ideas and styles of the Vienna Secession and the Wiener Werkstätte.

Jacqueline soon had a large number of clients, many of them German, and her reputation as a designer of distinction was beginning to grow. In 1930, in an article on her work by Dr Hans Von Ankwicz, published in the influential German publication *Deutsche Kunst und Dekoration*, she is described as a 'front-runner of the Hoffmann school' who 'currently dominates the design of textiles, particularly prints'. Ankwicz considered her two most original designs to be a cushion cover for the Wiener Werkstätte composed of white, black and red squares with a design of silver feathers springing across, and a very individualistic multi-toned fabric for deckchairs. The article also has a photographic portrait of the young Jacqueline that shows the ethereal and fragile quality of her beauty.[23]

Friends often recall her apparent unworldliness, which came across clearly in her attitude to her work, which she referred to, with reverence and affection, as 'My Designs'.[24] Certainly her 'Designs' – her creations – were very precious to her and, true to her inheritance from the Secession and the Werkstätte, she never recognised any boundary between the fine and decorative arts. Ankwicz refers to her as 'a woman with a rich and spiritual culture' whose artwork and message, he suggests, will reach a new level, her distinct creations influencing all areas of design.[25]

Jacqueline first went to Paris in 1930, armed with letters of introduction from, amongst others, Josef Hoffmann. She spent a greater part of that year making contact with the prestigious fashion houses, for whom she designed and produced unique hand-printed lengths of fabric, particularly silk. Amongst the couturiers from whom she received commissions were Chanel, Lanvin, Worth, Schiaparelli and Paul Poiret.[26] She also designed furnishing fabrics for the distinguished textile manufacturer, Rodier.[27]

Earlier that year Jacqueline had met her future husband Jacques Groag. She later recalled she had decided to spend the Christmas of 1930 in Paris and that Jacques had subsequently turned up to ensure she returned with him to Vienna the following January.[28] The tightening of the economic depression in the early 1930s and the growing anti-Semitism of the fast deteriorating political situation in Austria contributed considerably to the closure of the Wiener Werkstätte in 1932. Despite this Jacqueline's client group continued to grow, particularly in Germany where there was still a large and expanding mass market. She also continued to travel seeking new clients, not only to Paris but also New York,[29] all of which served to enhance her reputation internationally.

Jacques and Jacqueline first met at a masked ball. Such balls were central to the Viennese social whirl, of which the Werkstätte was very much part. It is probable that the ball where they met was the 'Evening in Haiti', an especially fantastical fancy dress masked ball organised by the Wiener Werkstätte. Jacques had an exceptionally fond memory of the evening which he later recalled in London: Jacqueline was 'particularly beautiful, she had created a dress out of red and gold cloth, with golden sandals, and in her jet-black hair she wore a Japanese bowl with a golden crest'.[30] Jacqueline later told Margaret Timmers that Jacques said he had fallen instantly in love with her when they met at a masked ball in Vienna.[31]

Although they became engaged in 1931, they did not marry until 1937. In the intervening years they were a well-known and respected couple in the intellectual and artistic life of the city. Jacques had been a pupil and assistant of the famous proto-Modernist architect Adolf Loos and through him had met many of the leading figures of the Viennese Modern Movement. When, as a very young man, he had first arrived in the city to study, he was introduced by his older sister, Trude, to the composers Arnold Schoenberg, Alban Berg and Anton Webern, all of whom became his friends.

Above Portrait of Jacqueline (when she was still known as Hilde Blumberger) by Jacobi Bildnis, published in 1930 in *Deutsche Kunst und Dekoration*.

Right *First Night*, a roller-printed rayon *Marocain*, produced by F.W. Grafton, 1946. A design based on a drawing of an opening at the Paris Opera House, 1937, conceived originally for Schiaparelli. Gerald Holtom wrote that Jacques and Jacqueline could be clearly distinguished in the audience. Coll. H. Kirk Brown & Jill A. Wiltse.

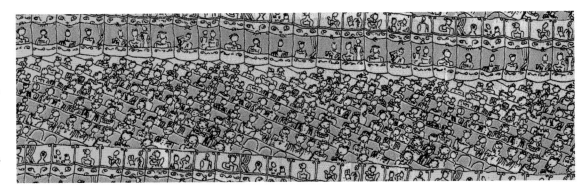

Amongst others he knew very well were the painters Oska Kokoschka, a protégé of Adolf Loos; Egon Schiele; the theatre director Max Reinhardt; Sigmund Freud; the musicians Artur Schnabel and Artur Rubenstein and the philosopher, Ludwig Wittgenstein, an admirer of Loos.[32] To this heady mix Jacqueline brought

Above Jacques and Jacqueline, Prague, circa 1939. In the background is the armoire Kate Irvine recalls Jacques restoring, on top of which stand Jacqueline's dolls. Groag family collection

Right Jacqueline modelling in a fashion feature for the Sunday supplement of the *Wiener Tag* newspaper. A photomontage by the Modernist photographer Trude Fleischmann, 1936.

[32] Stefan Buzas, Jacques Groag Obituary, 1962, Groag Archive, AAD.

[33] Anscombe/Groag.

[34] Ibid.

[35] *Der Sonntag,* supplement of the newspaper *Der Wiener Tag,* 2 August 1936.

[36] Ankwicz.

[37] Gordon Russell, Jacques Groag obituary 1962, AAD.

[38] Kate Irvine, interview with the authors, May 2008.

[39] Timmers.

[40] Prokop, pp.55-59.

[41] Contemporary photograph in possession of Karin Williger's son, Zac Manassah.

[42] Stefan Buzas, Memorial lecture on the life and work of Jacques Groag, 1962, AAD

her connections and friendships with Josef Hoffmann, the celebrated teachers of the Kunstgewerbeschule and the designers of the Werkstätte. Jacqueline and Jacques also had many friends from the Bauhaus, particularly her hero Paul Klee, 'whose childlike nature, naivety and simplicity was,' she felt, 'so close to my own soul'.[33] She collected all of Klee's books and particularly regretted not having paid more attention when she attended a lecture he gave at the Österreichischer Werkbund, of which Jacques was a member, where she drifted off, something she blamed on her 'very dreamy nature'.[34]

In the early to mid-1930s they were indeed a golden couple. At that time, with her exceptional good looks, large green eyes, jet black hair and delicate, almost waif-like physique, Jacqueline was a popular model with painters and photographers. She often sat for the Modernist photographer Trude Fleischmann, who used her as the model for a remarkable series of images in a fashion feature in the 2nd August 1936 issue of *Der Sonntag*.[35] Fleischmann was another member of the Groags' wide circle of friends. With their lively personalities and attractive looks, Jacques and Jacqueline were always welcome at the fashionable gatherings of the Viennese artistic and intellectual elite. But Vienna was not the only setting for relaxation and pleasure. Amongst the various

country retreats and coastal resorts they frequented, a particular favourite of Jacqueline's was the island of Arbe,[36] situated off the Dalmatian coast of Croatia, a former territory of the old Hapsburg Empire. She continued to use the island's scenery and townscapes as a source of inspiration for her work for many years.

Despite Jacques' commitment to the architecture of the Modern Movement, he retained, throughout his life, a fine appreciation of the decorative and the fantastical. Later, in London, he vividly described to Gordon Russell the dramatic impact on him and the pleasure he derived as a young boy from seeing the Archbishop of Prague in his splendid coach, attended by outriders carrying torches, as he drove to his palace on a winter's evening.[37] Kate Irvine, daughter of the Groags' close friend, the émigré architect and exhibition designer, Stefan Buzas, remembers as a young girl visiting the Groags and the immense patience and trouble that Jacques took to explain to her the various effects that different colours of paint had when placed side by side on a highly decorated baroque armoire he was restoring.[38] The armoire has also been recalled by others for its surprising presence in that austere Modernist interior.[39]

Such vignettes show the depth of the creative empathy that existed between Jacques and Jacqueline. Of their time together in Vienna in the 1930s, Ursula Prokop observes that both artists must have worked together at an early stage, for all Jacques' interiors incorporated fabric covered panelling, in all probability based on designs drawn up by Jacqueline; these panels became a virtual trademark.[40] This co-operative approach to their work is a reflection of the Secessionists' ideal of the Gesamtkunstwerk. In photographs of the studio-bedsitting room that Karin Williger's parents commissioned for her from Jacques in 1937, the surprisingly decorative floral textiles used in such a strict modernist interior were the work of Jacqueline.[41] There was to be later, in London, a prestigious example of an integrated interior by them for the Festival of Britain.

In his memorial lecture on Jacques' work, following his death in 1962, Stefan Buzas quotes from a lecture given by Jacques on design and architecture, in which he expressed his belief that 'by its spiritual radiation, by smile and charm, architecture has to bring joy to the man of the machine age, not utility only'.[42]

Such animatism has a long history in mid-European Jewish folklore and tradition, and is one of the themes of Bruce Chatwin's novel, *Utz,* which is set in Prague. In the book Chatwin illustrates a Jewish notion of the creative process

Below Design for furnishing fabric inspired by the Isle of Arbe on the Dalmatian Coast, published in *Deutsche Kunst und Dekoration,* 1930.

Above opposite Jacqueline, circa 1933, photographed with her dolls. Courtesy of the Victoria and Albert Museum

Below opposite One of Jacqueline's painted wooden dolls made by the Werkstätten Hagenauer 1925, and later given by Jacqueline to her great friend Stefan Buzas' daughter, Kate. Collection Kate Irvine

43 Bruce Chatwin, *Utz,* Jonathan Cape Ltd, 1988, London, p.33.

44 Wolf Pascheles, *Galerie der Sippurim,* published by Wolf Pascheles of Prague, 1847.

45 Chatwin.

46 Thomas Weiss, lecture, attended by Geoff Rayner, given by Karin Williger's brother Thomas, then head of the Camphill Rudolf Steiner Schools in Britain, 1970, at the Alternative Society meeting place, Gandolf's Garden. According to Weiss, there was then a belief at the Steiner Schools that their compost heaps were animated with the life force by building them around various animal parts, loosely arranged in the form of a human figure.

47 Irvine.

48 AAD.

49 Ibid.

50 Ibid.

51 Ibid.

52 Ibid.

53 *Furnishings From Britain,* National Trade Press Ltd, 1949-1950, p.74.

54 Prokop, p.111.

55 Ibid. pp.100-107.

– the power of animating the inanimate – with the legend of how in the sixteenth century the great Rabbi Loew, the 'undisputed leader of Prague Jewry in the reign of the Emperor Rudolf', created and gave life to an artificial man, Yossel the Golem, whom he had formed from the mud of the river Vltava.[43]

It was said Loew had made the Golem to defend the Prague ghetto from anti-Semitic attacks. In doing so Loew was imitating the original biblical act of creation in Genesis 2, when '…the Lord God formed man of the dust of the ground, and breathed into his nostrils the breath of life; and man became a living soul'. Only very holy people close to God had such power. A Golem servant was seen as the ultimate symbol of wisdom and holiness:[44]

All Golem legends derived from an ancient Jewish belief that any righteous man could create the world by repeating, in an order prescribed by the Cabbala, the letters of the secret name of God. 'Golem' means 'unformed' or 'uncreated' in Hebrew.[45]

As imaginative and creative Jewish children brought up in Prague, it is probable that Jacques or Jacqueline, or both, would have known such old tales and legends. Jacqueline certainly animated her 'designs' with vitality and energy, and endowed them with the attributes of life, an imaginative concept she shared with Jacques. Such esoteric ideas and mysticism were fashionable amongst many artists and intellectuals in Vienna in the early twentieth century and are particularly exemplified in the teaching of Rudolf Steiner and the Anthroposphical Society and the Theosophical Movement.[46]

Jacqueline had several sources of inspiration which remained important to her throughout her life. The towns and landscapes of the island of Arbe have already been referred to, but of much greater significance were her dolls. Throughout her working life the dolls appear in endless permutations in her designs. Some of the actual dolls, now very battered and scuffed, still exist, a gift she unexpectedly made in her old age to Kate Irvine, presumably to ensure their longevity and safe keeping after her death.[47] They are refined versions of simple wooden Austrian peasant toys, possibly produced by the Wiener Werkstätte. One, however, is of a different design and is signed with the name of the distinguished Viennese company of metalworkers, the Werkstätten Hagenauer, and dated 1925. Modernist wooden toys were also produced at the Bauhaus and became the inspiration for many avant-garde toy makers in the 1920s and 1930s.

A beautiful photograph exists from about 1933 of Jacqueline holding her dolls with great

reverence.[48] They subsequently appear in her designs, in various guises. An article in *The Ambassador* magazine, 1946, illustrates a nursery textile for F.W. Grafton which features the dolls in their full glory, and they also appear in *Beauty Contest*, one of the textiles she designed for the Rayon Design Centre in 1948. They continue to re-appear in Jacqueline's work over the next twenty-five or so years, in the early 1950s wearing Austrian peasant headdresses and then as puppets in *Puppet Ballet*, a dress fabric from 1954 for Associated American Artists; in 1960 they decorate plastic laminates *Alexandretta* and *Lilliput*; become *Paper Dolls* in 1967 and in 1968 attend a *Garden Party* for Cavendish Textiles.

In the last year or so of her life she made a mock-up of a proposed limited edition book of the highlights of her life's work, in which she wrote on several blank pages, 'My Dolls'.[49] The dolls, without doubt, had an extremely deep emotional – almost spiritual – significance for her. Whether they represented the children she never had is debatable. Whatever they were or were not, they were certainly her 'Golems', companions she endowed with life through the medium of her designs. The depth of the dolls' strange significance for her and her identification with them is made apparent in a photograph of her in Vienna in the mid-1930s, where her hairstyle and makeup clearly resemble theirs.[50]

That Jacqueline and Jacques' relationship became the creative mainspring of their lives, an almost symbiotic union, was made manifest when they married and she became, instead of Hilde, Jacqueline to his Jacques. In a letter she sent to Stefan Buzas following Jacques' death in 1962, she wrote that 'his wonderful, never aging, youthful enthusiasm took me to spheres so high and so unearthly as no man ever did and no man can imagine'.[51]

Jacques' 'youthful' enthusiasm certainly appears to have paid dividends in terms of Jacqueline's work, for in 1931 she won a prestigious award at the Paris Exposition Coloniale Internationale for lace design and in 1933 a gold medal for textile design at the Milan Triennale.[52] They married in 1937, the year of the Paris World Fair, where Jacqueline was invited to exhibit her textiles in the Austrian Pavilion, designed by the architect and leading exhibition designer, Professor Carl Witzmann. By coincidence, also exhibiting textiles in the Austrian Pavilion was the pattern designer Marian Mahler, subsequently a successful textile designer in post-war Britain.[53] Both Jacqueline and Mahler's work was shown alongside that of some of the most celebrated Austrian designers and craftspeople of the twentieth century. Prominent amongst these were Josef Frank and Lucie Rie, both of whom were soon after declared 'non-Austrian' and forced to emigrate.[54] Jacqueline was awarded a gold medal at the fair for printed textile design, probably the last positive event of any significance in her and Jacques' lives in pre-war Europe.

In March the following year, 1938, the political unification of Austria and Germany, the *Anschluss*, occurred and the Nuremberg Race Laws were enforced to full effect in the Ostmark, the term used to denote the position of Austria within the greater German Reich. This was a life-threatening situation for Jews in Austria, which, amongst so much else, prevented them from practising any profession. Since the Groags were technically Czech citizens and held Czech passports, they were neither subject to the Austrian authorities nor the Race Laws and were able to emigrate to Czechoslovakia and save at least some of their possessions and a fair proportion of their work. They survived for about a year and a half in Prague, where Jacques managed to continue his work from an office in the old town.[55]

Both Jacques and Jacqueline received much help and support from friends and fellow émigrés from Vienna. Prominent amongst these was Jacques' good friend, the painter Oska

Left *Dolls Galore*, a design for printed cotton nursery fabric for F.W. Grafton, 1945.

Right Jacqueline, Vienna, circa 1936. Her highly made-up appearance resembles that of her dolls. Karin Williger distinctly remembered the finely pleated white culotte trousers that Jacqueline frequently wore at that time. Courtesy of the Victoria and Albert Museum

Kokoschka. Soon after 1933, in Germany, Kokoschka's name was already included on lists of persons proscribed by the Nazi state. He wisely left Vienna for Prague in 1934, where he set up the Oska Kokoschka League, an anti-Fascist group of artists. He subsequently obtained a Czech passport and became a personal friend of the President, Tomas Masaryk. In the autumn of 1938, following the Munich crisis and the secession of the Sudetenland from Czechoslovakia to Germany, Kokoschka, on the advice of his international contacts and his own shrewd, political nous, left Prague for London. The Groags, and many others like them, remained for only a few months more, still hoping for a permanent refuge, until the spring of 1939 when Germany extended its occupation to the whole of Czechoslovakia. Just before the Czech border closed Jacques and Jacqueline were once more forced to flee. This time their destination was Britain, which they reached after a long and adventurous journey, without visas, via Paris and Holland.[56] Jacqueline often later joked they were, metaphorically, 'on the last boat out'. Later Professor Charles Reilly sadly wrote of Jacqueline's situation in 1939 that…

from Paris to New York it was but a short step, as it always is to the really gifted. There her work was beginning to sell and to be sought after by the journals interested in such things, when the war cloud burst.[57]

1939-1945: Emigration, London and the Second World War

In the late 1930s Britain would have appeared an inviting and sympathetic destination for émigrés like the Groags. Adolf Loos and the philosopher Ludwig Wittgenstein were well-known anglophiles, and for Hoffmann, Moser and other members of the Vienna Secession, England was renowned as the home of William Morris, C.R. Ashbee and other heroes of the Arts and Crafts Movement. Even greater admiration was reserved for the Scottish architect Charles Rennie Mackintosh and his wife Margaret Macdonald, whose work had been a major influence on that of the Wiener Werkstätte. The German architect, Hermann Muthesius, at the behest of the German government, had published his seminal work *Das englische Haus* in 1904, which, from Le Corbusier and the Bauhaus to the Secession and the Wiener Werkstätte, had a profound influence on European Modernism. From the elegant refinement of its Georgian squares and terraces, to the leafy tranquillity of the Garden Suburbs inspired by the precepts of the Arts and Crafts Movement, and its long history of parliamentary democracy, Britain was seen by many as a humane and civilised place of refuge from the political maelstrom of 1930s mainland Europe.

The British way of life seems to have particularly appealed to those of the Austrian exodus and the Groags found many friends and acquaintances from Vienna already in London. Sigmund Freud and his family had arrived earlier in 1939; Ludwig Wittgenstein was to remain in Britain until his death in 1951 and Oska Kokoschka and the ceramicist Lucie Rie, like the Freud family and numerous others, subsequently took British citizenship. However, in August 1939 the reality of Britain was very different from the safe haven hoped for by Jacques and Jacqueline. On arrival in London they found themselves members of an uprooted group of disorientated and anxious ex-patriots in a country shaken to its roots and preparing to fight for its life.[58]

Although the Groags' flight to Britain appears sudden and dramatic, some preparations must have been made in advance, for they were all but 'met off the boat'[59] by Gordon Russell and Jack Pritchard and their cause taken up by influential members of the British design fraternity. Prominent amongst these were not only Russell and Pritchard but also the doyen of British architecture, Charles Reilly. The Groags were immediately given temporary shelter in the London home of a former patron of Jacques from Vienna, Hans Moller. Jacques had worked with Adolf Loos in 1927 on a commission from Moller for a villa in Vienna's Starkfriedgasse.[60] Following the Mollers' departure for Palestine in the summer of 1940, Jacques and Jacqueline were given a permanent apartment by Jack Pritchard in his Isokon Lawn Road flats in Hampstead.

In late 1939 there was little demand for the Groags' talents, although some commissions for furniture and interior design were given to Jacques by the John Lewis Partnership. This firm had shown great concern for émigrés and provided them with much practical assistance,[61] so it was probably partly in gratitude that in 1943 a group of émigré artists held a prestigious exhibition in John Lewis' heavily bombed headquarters, in London's Oxford Street, entitled 'For Freedom'.[62] It was at this exhibition that Oska Kokoschka's well-known political allegories were first shown.

Jacques' commissions for John Lewis in 1939 and 1940 would have been obtained partly through the good offices of his Viennese friend, the émigré architect and interior designer, Franz Singer, who on arrival in London in 1938 had been commissioned by John Lewis to work on the interior of their flagship store in Oxford

Street.[63] However, it is important in this context to know that one of Jacques' and Jacqueline's most influential patrons, Charles Reilly, was a personal friend of John Spedan Lewis and, between 1925 and 1945, adviser on architecture and design to the Partnership. He was consultant architect between 1934 and 1939 for both the rebuilding of Peter Jones – the John Lewis store in Sloane Square – and the Oxford Street headquarters. Both stores, now considered amongst the finest examples of British Modernism, were the work of Reilly's former student, William Crabtree. In a memorandum from John Spedan Lewis to the Acting Director of Building dated 24 December 1941, Lewis writes:

…we have at present no work that suits Mr Groag sufficiently well, but that we are by no means without hope of being able to offer him commissions at a later stage in the designing of these buildings in London and elsewhere but at present we cannot give him a continuous retainer.[64]

In 1939 Singer commissioned a large photomontage as a mural for the restaurant of the Oxford Street store from Karin Williger's employer and lover Robert Haas.[65] Either Reilly or Singer would have introduced Jacqueline to the John Lewis management, which marked the beginning of her professional relationship with the store that was to last from the early 1940s through to the late 1970s. Subsequently, commenting on these early years in Britain, Jacqueline said that, although some, like the John Lewis management, were willing to help, most of the English did not understand her work, which they seemed completely unable to 'read'.[66] Despite this she was extremely grateful for the refuge and the help she and Jacques had received, and, paraphrasing Pope Gregory the Great, she described the English as 'Angels not Angles'.[67] Gordon Russell was one of those who also gave practical help by obtaining for Jacques a place on the board of the wartime Utility Furniture Advisory Committee, but Jacques' work never regained the status it held in Vienna in the 1920s and 1930s.

For Jacqueline, however, this was very much her moment. Perhaps surprisingly for a Modernist architect, Charles Reilly was amongst the most vocal of her supporters. In the sphere of architecture he had been a power in the land, a major figure in twentieth century British architecture who had been largely responsible for establishing the teaching of architecture as a university subject. He and his son Paul, later to become Director of the Council of Industrial Design, were pre-war contacts of the Groags.

Paul had studied in Germany before the war and had travelled extensively in Europe and during the war both he and his father gave help to many émigrés. Already an admirer and advocate of Jacques' work, Charles Reilly took up Jacqueline's cause and in October 1942 published an article in *Art and Industry* on her work,[68] for which he had the greatest admiration. Like many before he also had a keen appreciation of her personal charms, referring in the article to those who 'have the good fortune to know Madame Groag', and how he finds her ' a kind and beautiful person in every way'. He also makes reference to 'the world of the imagination in which she lives'. His appreciation of her designs reaches its culmination when he writes that a particular fabric, 'Starlight, with its interweaving of delicate chains, suggests to me marvellous and mysterious talks under the stars. I cannot remember designs for fabrics affecting me in this way before'.[69]

Apart from Reilly's great personal enthusiasm for Jacqueline, the article draws attention to the fact that, despite wartime constraints, 'a few wise and far-seeing firms are buying up her designs at exhibitions, such as the one at the Cotton Board held a little time back at the Central Art Gallery in Manchester'. This exhibition, held in 1941, was organised by James Cleveland Belle, Director of the newly formed Cotton Board, with Gerald Holtom as exhibition designer. Jacqueline's work would have been shown alongside designs by leading British artists such as Graham Sutherland, Paul Nash, John Piper, Frank Dobson and Duncan Grant. One of Cleveland Belle's and the Cotton Board's principal tasks was to promote and maintain a high profile for the textile industry in the middle of what Reilly called in his article 'a desperate war in which our very existence is at stake'. Although there was an extremely limited printing of textiles for the home market, there was less constraint on those destined for export: a source of badly needed cash for the war effort and an effective tool of propaganda.

Following soon after Reilly's article another on Jacqueline appeared in the January 1943 issue of *The Textile Manufacturer*.[70] Jacqueline's work is again the principal subject of 'Motifs in Textile Design' which, in its admiration for her and the references to 'slav blood' etc, owes much to Reilly's. She is presented in both articles as a Czech designer, with little, if any, reference to her Viennese background and none at all to her Jewishness. One purpose of both articles was, apparently, to mitigate against any xenophobic reaction towards refugees. The article in *The Textile*

56 Ibid.

57 Charles Reilly, 'Design For Textiles, The Work of Jacqueline Groag', *Art & Industry*, October 1942, p.96.

58 Buzas, Jacques Groag obituary.

59 Timmers.

60 Prokop, pp.105.

61 Ibid.

62 The John Lewis Partnership archive.

63 Ibid.

64 Ibid.

65 Ibid.

66 Anscombe/Groag.

67 Ibid.

68 Reilly.

69 Ibid.

70 Anon, 'Motifs in Textile Design', *The Textile Manufacturer*, January 1943.

Above The Cavendish Square façade of the new John Lewis flagship store, 1939, architect William Crabtree. Photograph mid-1950s. Courtesy of the John Lewis Partnership Archive Collection

Designs exhibited at the
Milan Triennale, 1933,
which won Jacqueline a gold
medal for textile design.
Courtesy of the Victoria and
Albert Museum

Opposite *Art & Industry* cover, October 1942, a design by 'Madame' Groag.

Below left *Starlight*, a design for fabric by Jacqueline, much admired by Charles Reilly and illustrated in his *Art & Industry* article, 1942.

Below centre Textile design published in *The Textile Manufacturer*, 1943.

Below right Textile design, *Slavonika* illustrated in *Art & Industry* 1942.

71 Ibid.

72 Anscombe/Groag.

73 Lucienne Day, interview with the authors, 1999.

74 Ibid.

75 Lesley Jackson, *Robin & Lucienne Day: Pioneers of Contemporary Design*, Mitchell Beazley, London, 2001. Lucienne repeated this information in an interview with the authors in August 2008.

Manufacturer also refers to 'two small exhibitions of Czech manufacturers a short time ago...', in which Jacqueline had taken part, and that showed 'pre-war refugees from Middle Europe had, even in wartime, made a contribution to technique and to design and style in various productions likely to do a great deal of future good for this country'.[71]

No reference is made to who the Czech manufacturers or the exhibition organisers were but, at that time, there was only one refugee textile manufacture of Czech origin in Britain of sufficient status and dynamism to have organised such exhibitions. Ascher was a company recently set up by the émigrés Zika and Lida Ascher to produce textiles for the upper end of the fashion industry. Given Jacqueline's international status and the Aschers' ambition and publicity skills, it is most probable that, within such a small ex-patriot community, she was invited to take part in some early Ascher promotions.

By 1943 Jacqueline was becoming well known and respected within the war-straitened British textile industry and her work much sought after. She has described how a member of the Calico Printers Association (almost certainly F.W. Grafton) tried unsuccessfully to obtain her agreement to a seven year contract, commencing from the end of the war, for a range of textiles for the couture trade.[72] For a pattern designer, achieving such success in Britain was then a remarkable feat. Unlike Continental Europe and the United States, 1940s Britain generally considered 'Design' somewhat esoteric and unnecessary. It was largely a peripheral activity: the interest of architects, artists, talented gentlemen of independent means and well-heeled ladies with either some training in the Arts and Crafts or a flare for such things. Although, for nearly a century, architects and other members of the design conscious middle classes had been attempting to educate 'the masses' to appreciate what they considered 'good design', there had been hardly any serious recognition given to the potentially important role of the professional designer working within mainstream manufacturing industries. Any whiff of what the cognoscenti then considered commercial and populist was necessarily eschewed as vulgar.

The textile designer Lucienne Day recalled that, when a novice in the 1940s, it was the practice for a freelance designer to send packets of designs to the textile converters or manufacturers. At best they would choose one or two and return the rest with a cheque for those selected. The going rate for a design was somewhere between thirty shillings to four guineas which seems to have been determined by whether it was for dress or furnishing fabric.[73] Designers were rarely credited with a design and, working freelance or in-house, had a lowly status. Lucienne remembered with some amusement and satisfaction how she was probably the first person to have 'Designer' as a profession on her passport, which caused some confusion and raised eyebrows when she went through customs.[74]

Jacqueline experienced none of these problems. With her pre-war status as a distinguished designer in Europe and the United States, and the support and respect of the British design fraternity, she was in a privileged position. For the duration of the war she mainly supplied designs for the export trade. Amongst her principal clients were F.W. Grafton, Gerald Holtom, Hill Brown and Co, Moygashel and Cavendish Textiles, a division of the John Lewis Partnership. A majority of the textiles of the Wiener Werkstätte had been for fashion and this always remained an important part of Jacqueline's oeuvre. Unlike many British textile designers, she never regarded the designing of dress fabrics as a secondary activity. Lucienne Day, for example, as a tyro designer in the later 1940s, resented what she considered to be the disdain shown to freelance designers by the notoriously fickle men who ran the much more cut-throat dress fabric trade, in contrast to those of the more gentlemanly world of furnishing fabrics.[75] However, because of her and Robin

ART AND INDUSTRY

OCTOBER 1942
ONE SHILLING

Day's incomes from teaching at that time, Lucienne felt able to take 'a rather snooty line' towards those involved in the 'rag trade'.[76]

By the mid-1940s Jacqueline was arguably the most influential designer of surface pattern in Britain. She ran her own studio from a prestigious address at 2 Albany Terrace, Regent's Park. employed Karin Williger as her assistant and was regularly visited by representatives of the leading textile converters and manufacturers, either to buy or to commission designs from her. In May 1945 the Central Institute of Art and Design and the National Gallery jointly held an influential exhibition, *Historical and British Wallpapers*, at the Suffolk Galleries, London. Considering the limitations of wartime restrictions, the exhibition's catalogue was a particularly well-designed and illustrated colour production, which advocated the future use of pattern and colour in post-war homes. In the *Contemporary* section, designs by artists such as Graham Sutherland and Edward Bawden were shown alongside the work of designers. Jacqueline exhibited at least three designs, one of which was a beautiful, slightly reworked, floral pattern from 1929, which still remains fresh in style and concept.[77]

1945-1950: *Britain Can Make It*, The Rayon Design Centre, the Kardomah Restaurants

In 1945, the rather tired trade journal, *International Textiles,* was transformed by the émigrés Hans and Elsbeth Juda into an influential post-war export magazine, *The Ambassador*. The following year the magazine ran several features on Jacqueline. 'Prehistoric Topics' was exclusively illustrated with her designs and 'Jacqueline Groag Designs' was devoted to her work. Throughout the later 1940s examples of Jacqueline's work were regularly featured in the magazine and she was commissioned to design covers for the December 1948 and the February and August 1950 issues. Elsbeth Juda, recalling Jacqueline at that time, remembers her as not conventionally beautiful, but 'extremely chic and elegant in an unconventional way'.[78]

The *Britain Can Make It* exhibition of 1946 was the first and, apart from the Festival of

[76] Interviews with Geoff Rayner and Richard Chamberlain, August 2008.

[77] Victoria and Albert Museum, Department of Prints and Drawings (DPP).

[78] Elsbeth Juda, interview with the authors, May 2008.

[79] The Council of Industrial Design Annual Report, 1946-47.

[80] *Britain Can Make It* (BCMI) Exhibition Catalogue, Council of Industrial Design, HMSO, 1946, p.35.

[81] Timmers.

Britain, the biggest design extravaganza of the post-war era. Held in the galleries of the Victoria and Albert Museum, which had been emptied for the duration of the war, the exhibition opened on 24th September 1946 and by the end of December had been visited by 1,432,546 people.[79] An ambitious blockbuster survey of British goods and manufacturers, the exhibition was a victorious propaganda exercise whose aims were to demonstrate the high quality of British industrial design and so boost the vital export trade, while simultaneously lifting the morale of a public long deprived of consumer goods and desperate for luxury and glamour. Wartime restrictions were still in place, however, and most of the goods so enticingly displayed were for export only, prototypes of what might be, or goods which would be available to the public at some later, but unspecified, date. A cynical and war-weary public wryly renamed the exhibition, *Britain Can Make It but Britain Can't Have It*.

Three of Jacqueline's textiles for the John Lewis Partnership are listed in the exhibition's catalogue.[80] There are also other textiles listed for companies she is known to have done much work for but that are not credited to any designer. The well-known fashion textile *First Night*, produced by F.W. Grafton, was almost certainly exhibited and was subsequently first

published in the December 1946 issue of *The Ambassador*. Its design was a witty interpretation of a first night at the Paris Opera, originally designed in 1937, it is thought, for Schiaparelli.[81] *First Night* was also marketed in America where it was known as *Gala Night*. Another probable candidate is a printed cotton, circa 1945, patterned with an allegory of peace, with doves holding olive branches, green shoots sprouting in pots, toppling castles from a chess set and sunflowers with smiling faces.

The years between 1946 and 1956 were the high point of Jacqueline's post-war career. In 1946 she received the accolade of one of her dress fabrics being chosen by the couturier Edward Molyneux for a collection of dresses he

Three Cover designs by Jacqueline for *The Ambassador* magazine, published in December 1948, February and August 1950. The 1948 cover was subsequently available as a printed dress fabric produced by F.W. Grafton.

had designed for Her Majesty the Queen when Princess Elizabeth. Photographs of the Princess wearing the dress were published in the popular magazine *Illustrated* in September 1946.[82] The fabric, produced by F.W. Grafton, was a version of Jacqueline's classic tulip motif that could have come straight from the Wiener Werkstätte itself. Molyneux had earlier used fabrics designed by the Czech émigré Lida Ascher for his 1942 export couture dress collection and in 1947 he used a textile, designed by the painter Gerald Wilde, from Ascher's celebrated collection of artist designed textiles, for Princess Elizabeth's wardrobe for the Royal family's tour of South Africa.[83] It is probable that the dress made from Jacqueline's tulip fabric was also part of the same collection. Once again there is a tantalizing near convergence of Jacqueline's and the Aschers' professional activities.

Jacques and Jacqueline received British citizenship in 1947 and that year became Members of the Society of Industrial Artists. The June 1947 issue of *Art and Industry* contains an article by the textile manufacturer and designer Gerald Holtom, 'The Printed Fabric, Designs by Jacqueline Groag, MSIA', in which, apart from his enthusiasm for Jacqueline's work, Holtom discusses at some length the history of emigrant craftsmen in Britain and the importation of alien concepts and styles. He finds that although the

…fruits of original thought are often at first received with hostility and misunderstanding, it is very much to the credit therefore of certain enterprising textile printers in this country that they recognised both the originality and the value of the work of Madame Jacqueline Groag. The result is that British textile is happily enriched. But let me first of all dispose of a false notion, which is widely held today about the employment of foreign designers and technicians in England. Many people consider that such employment means the introduction of ideas and motifs strange to our tradition. That this need not be so may be proved from our history.'[84]

This justification of immigration is an echo of both Charles Reilly's article and that in *The Textile Manufacturer*. In those, however, a greater emphasis is placed on Jacqueline's Czech origins, which Holtom ignores. In the 1940s, Austria's relationship with Germany was considered, at the very least, dubious and Jacqueline's Viennese background is hardly ever referred to; her Jewishness never at all. Whatever Holtom optimistically felt 'may be proved from our history', Lytton Strachey conversely, writing of the 'hideous tragedy' of the downfall of Elizabeth I's Portuguese

Above left Three fabrics designed by Jacqueline for F.W. Grafton and Hill Brown and published in Gerald Holtom's article in *Art & Industry*, 1947.

Above right Princess Elizabeth, wearing a dress made with one of Jacqueline's Wiener Werkstätte inspired designs, 'Tulip', for F.W. Grafton, 1946.

Opposite Pen and ink drawing by Karin Williger of Susan Cox at Jacqueline's Albany Terrace apartment, circa 1946. Courtesy of Joanna Cox

82 The cover of *Illustrated*, September 1946.

83 Photograph in *Illustrated*, April 1947.

84 Gerald Holtom, 'The Printed Fabric – Designs By Jacqueline Groag', *Art & Industry*, June 1947, pp.174-179.

85 Lytton Strachey, *Elizabeth and Essex: A Tragic History*, Penguin Books Edition, 1950, reprinted 1985, pp.48-62.

86 Susan Cox, letter to Anthony Cox, 1945, now in the possession of their daughter, Joanna Cox.

87 Irvine.

physician-in-chief, Dr Ruy Lopez, says that Lopez had

… obtained, in spite of professional jealousy and racial prejudice, a large practice among persons of distinction, … he reached the highest place in his profession … it was only natural that there should have been murmurs against a Jewish foreigner who had outdone his English rivals.[85]

Over four hundred years ago these 'murmurs', to the dismay of Elizabeth and her ministers, eventually ended in Lopez's unjust imprisonment, torture and execution. Like Lopez, Jacqueline was a successful émigré Jew and a Christian convert, but mercifully no such horrors could be visited on her or her fellow émigrés in Britain in the 1940s. Although anti-Semitism had by then been largely driven underground, it was still widely prevalent and 'murmurs' may well have contributed to the erosion of her later career and subsequent effacing of her reputation. At the time neither the jealousy, anti-Semitism or xenophobic attitudes that Reilly's, Holtom's and *The Textile Manufacturer's* articles were clearly intended to refute, or the trauma of wartime emigration, had any apparent effect on Jacqueline or her work. The same was not so for Jacques.

During the war Jacqueline's studio was in an apartment in Albany Terrace, near London's Regent's Park. Her assistant, Karin Williger, had a room there that she used as a studio-bedsitting room and there was a spare room for guests. Jacqueline moved her studio in 1945, but Karin stayed on, sharing the apartment with her friend Susan Cox. In a letter that year to her husband, the architect Anthony Cox, then serving in the army in India, Susan described the Albany Terrace apartment and its recent history. In the letter she recalls 'Mr and Mrs Groag, who were friends of 'Stef's' (the émigré architect Stefan Buzas) who, like the Groags, was then living in the Isokon Lawn Road flats. Apparently the Albany Terrace apartment had originally been intended as a home for the Groags, who, Susan wrote:

… have been trying for a long time to move somewhere larger than their Lawn Rd flat,…at the last minute Mr G, who has been very ill and is now very nervy, jibbed at the noise of the Marylebone Road traffic, and instead of taking the whole flat, Mrs G took the nicest room as her studio and suggested that Karin, who was going to work with her, should have the adjoining room…[86]

'Very ill' and 'very nervy' are the operative words here. Stefan Buzas' daughter, Kate Irvine, who from a very young child knew Jacques and Jacqueline well, describes him as a 'delicate plant' who had not transplanted to England very successfully. He was a fragile personality, who seemed to her, as a teenager, deeply depressed.[87] In the memorial lecture

Over page A modified version of Jacqueline's textile design of urns and columns for the Rayon Design Centre, produced commercially by David Whitehead, 1951. Collection H. Kirk Brown III and Jill A. Wiltse

[88] Buzas, Jacques Groag obituary, AAD.

[89] Reilly.

[90] *The Textile Manufacturer.*

[91] Toni del Renzio, Dennis Lennon's biographical entry in *Contemporary Designers,* ed. Ann Lee Morgan, Macmillan Publishers Ltd, London, 1984, pp.357-358.

Buzas gave in 1962 on Jacques, he sadly recalled Jacques' disappointment in England.[88] Despite his formidable pre-war reputation as an architect and the help he had received from friends such as Gordon Russell, Jacques' career failed to prosper. His later years were spent fighting increasing psychological problems and Jacqueline, perforce, became the principal breadwinner and bearer of the burdens of daily life. It was not until the 1950s that the pressures of life as émigrés finally eased and Jacques and Jacqueline were able to move to a house in Clifton Hill in the St John's Wood area of London. After the traumas of emigration and war, stability and continuity were essential to them and they continued to live there together until Jacques' death in 1962.

By 1947 Jacqueline had made a number of influential friends and allies in the design world. Prominent amongst these was the Russian émigré architect and exhibition designer Misha Black, co-founder with Milner Grey in 1945 of the Design Research Unit (DRU), the first British design consultancy. Another was the émigré Viennese interior, exhibition and industrial designer Gaby Schreiber. Both gave a series of important commissions to Jacqueline at the end of the 1950s and throughout the 1960s, which became the mainstay of her later career. The first prestigious project she was involved with in Britain, however, was the commission she received in 1948 from the architect Dennis Lennon for textiles and colour schemes for the new Rayon Design Centre in London's West End.

For Jacqueline such collaborations between architects, designers and artists in a synthesis of architecture and the fine and applied arts, the Gesamtkunstwerk, had been a familiar part of her work in Vienna. Throughout the 1930s she and Jacques had successfully co-operated on the interiors of his architectural projects in Austria, and Josef Hoffmann, whom she considered the greatest influence on her work, had founded the Wiener Werkstätte on such a premise. Charles Reilly wrote of Jacqueline in 1942 that:

one of the charming things she used to do, both in Prague and in Vienna, which is not a general practice yet in this country, was not only to make the designs for, but to print with hand blocks her own curtains for architects, so that these latter could put new and unique curtains into their own and their clients houses… I can imagine nothing more interesting than to ask Jacqueline Groag to design and print for me special curtains for rooms according to their character, lighting and use and my own very varying temperament … apparently in Czechoslovakia and Austria this was not an unusual thing before the war.[89]

Commissions for exclusive hand-printed lengths of fabric created for a particular purpose had also formed the basis of Jacqueline's success with the Parisian couture houses. A fascinating window on her thinking on the design of textiles, their production and the manufacturing process, is given in the article on her work in *The Textile Manufacturer*:

Mrs Groag considers that the designer should design for the actual fabric, heavy or light, opaque or slightly transparent, matt or shiny. Indeed she made designs and hand-blocked printed them herself for curtains for particular rooms … the design has to be put on paper, but the paper should be forgotten and the technique considered of the method of production. Many designers think their work is spoiled during reproduction but Mrs Groag considers that the design is no good if it is not reproducible. After the design is born the designer should, if possible, go to the workshop, see the craftsmen, weaver or printer, explain, discuss and collaborate, going into details with great care and considering colour schemes. It would mean time and trouble but there would be benefit to all and the dormant paper sketch would become real and alive. The user wants beauty and the textile designer should try to provide lovely things for a harmonious life.[90]

The image of a design as a 'dormant paper sketch' which is 'born' from the hand of the designer and subsequently becomes 'real and alive' through the collaboration of designer and craftsman is a perfect example of the animatism with which Jacques and Jacqueline endowed their work. Equally, 'lovely' and 'harmonious' provide the key to Jacqueline's commission for the newly created Rayon Design Centre.

Dennis Lennon had been commissioned in 1948 to sympathetically convert a large eighteenth century house in Upper Grosvenor Street, in London's Mayfair district, as the headquarters and showcase for the rayon industry, considered in the early post-war years an essential part of the all important export trade. The house had an elaborate neo-classical interior, the plasterwork of the ceilings being especially decorative. Lennon's conversion was particularly notable for the overall design plan for the new interior that was:

…meticulously pursued without any visible conflict with the equally meticulous respect for the existing building. Indeed the two were brought together by the sensitive colouring of the plasterwork, which was in turn related to the colours used for the furniture and furnishings.[91]

Jacqueline was commissioned to design textiles for the interiors whose colours and designs would harmonise with and reflect those of the neo-classical plasterwork. She designed a number of textiles for various rooms, one of which had architectural motifs of urns and columns incorporated in its design. A modified version of this, produced in 1951 by the textile manufacturer David Whitehead, has since

This page *Celia,* a wallpaper for John Line, 1955, and (attrib.) a printed cotton dress fabric, produced by Horrockses Fashions, circa 1958, both illustrating her naturalistic botanical style.

Opposite top Roller-printed rayon furnishing fabric by David Whitehead, 1952-3. Like so many of her designs this textile, based on a grid format, owes much to her time in Vienna with Josef Hoffman. Collection H. Kirk Brown III and Jill A. Wiltse

Opposite middle Detail of the textile designed by Jacqueline for the Press Room at the Festival of Britain's Regatta Restaurant, printed by the Calico Printers Association, 1951.

Opposite bottom Interior of the Press Room at the Regatta Restaurant, Festival of Britain, 1951.

92 *House and Garden,* 'Directory of Designers', Condé Nast Publications Ltd, September 1965, p.89.

93 *The Ambassador,* no 12, 1956, p.74.

94 AAD.

95 Misha Black, *Architecture, Art and Design in Unison, A Tonic For the Nation The Festival of Britain 1951,* ed. Mary Banham and Bevis Hillier, Thames and Hudson, 1976, p.83.

become an icon of post-war textile design. The design was achieved using a collage technique very like that of Matisse. Collage was a favourite medium of Jacqueline's, and forms the basis of much of the surviving original artwork for her designs. She would most often choose a small scale simple motif or image she had either drawn, painted or collaged, and multiply it by using PMTs (photo mechanical transfers), or other reprographic methods, until she had created a large number of repeats. These formed a base on which she would experiment with drawing and painting, applying colour washes and texture, overlaying coloured transparent plastic sheet, tissue papers, thin self adhesive plastics and coloured and metallic cards, in the process creating constructions which are small works of art. However, the final design presented to a client was more usually a smooth surfaced PMT of the original artwork, with hand applied colour washes, which eliminated most traces of the design process. Jacqueline's biography in the *House and Garden* 'Directory of Designers', 1965, notes 'she has constantly and ingeniously exploited the decorative possibilities of simple motifs, frequently in highly complex designs'.[92]

Although Jacqueline kept abreast of new materials and techniques, she continued to use traditional drawing and painting skills. Her delicate botanical and floral designs for dress fabrics and wallpapers are examples of the wide range of images and styles she used. An editorial in *The Ambassador* in 1956 considered that:

Few designers can move easily from abstract design to the representational and produce equally good work in both disciplines. Jacqueline Groag not only possesses this special gift but also the ability to abstract from life so that reality still exists in many of her patterns, but transformed by the wit and charm of her own personality.[93]

She was frequently commissioned to create a design for a particular situation or purpose and, although her involvement is sometimes not immediately obvious, her hand is nearly always discernible to those familiar with her work. Her working methods and aims, described in the article in *The Textile Manufacturer* in 1943, are extremely Modernist in their functionalist approach to pattern making, and nearly always related to the requirements of a particular situation or the particular properties of a material and method of production. The rational underlying grid structure of pattern design associated with Hoffmann is often apparent in Jacqueline's work, as is, paradoxically, the richness and eclecticism of her design sources which owe much to the influence of the Werkstätte.

Following her successful collaboration with Lennon for textiles for the Rayon Design Centre, Jacqueline received a commission from Misha Black of the DRU to work with him on a restyling of the Kardomah chain of restaurants and coffee shops. Black had been design consultant to the Kardomah cafés since 1936 and their style was held in high regard by Modernist architects and designers. The restyling of the chain between 1949 and 1950 was his last work for the company. Jacqueline's brief was to design the textiles and graphic design for the restaurants' and cafés' new interiors. The restyling was so successful it survived well into the mid-1960s. The design of a menu card in the Groag archive, for a Liverpool branch of the chain, continued using Jacqueline's graphic design until at least November 1966.[94] One of her textiles for the commission was published in *Designers in Britain*, 1951.

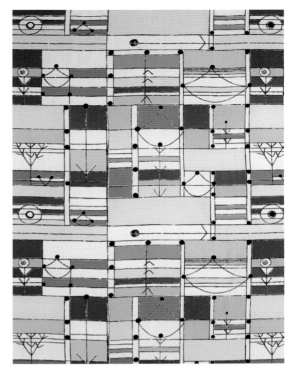

1951-1956: The Festival of Britain
David Whitehead and Associated
American Artists

As her commission for the Kardomah chain ended in 1950, Jacqueline began work on another, also from Black, for a textile for the Press Room of the Regatta Restaurant at the Festival of Britain. The Festival was a catch-all for many purposes. Ostensibly commemorating the centenary of the *Great Exhibition* in 1851, and thus recalling the apex of British political and economic world dominance, it was also in part a trade fair, showcasing British goods, as well as a celebration of the British way of life and its historical, artistic and scientific achievements. Above all, the Festival of Britain is probably best understood as a five month long party the British gave, both to congratulate themselves on their survival and victory in the Second World War and to relieve the drab austerity of the post-war era. Misha Black, one of the most distinguished exhibition designers of the period, had been appointed one of the three co-ordinating architects for the Festival, along with Ralph Tubbs and Hugh Casson, each of whom also gave themselves one building as a personal architectural and design task. Black later wrote that 'it was the lifeline to sanity, a specific to compensate for the tasks of co-ordination which demanded diplomacy and persuasion as much as perception. I chose the Regatta Restaurant and the Bailey Bridge across the Thames'.[95]

Jacqueline's textile for the Press Room was part of a larger commission Black had given to his own design consultancy, DRU, along with the contract for the exhibition design and

display for the Festival's *Dome of Discovery*. Ralph Tubbs was the architect of the *Dome*, but Black was co-ordinating designer of the exhibition within it. The exhibition was a 'story told in eight sections, each of which is concerned with one of the great provinces that together make up the universe'.[96] The eighth section, *The Living World*, was concerned with 'Britain's contribution to biological discovery'.[97]

The theme here is two fold – the idea of evolution and the study of living things in relation to their environment … The work of Charles Darwin is closely woven, as it must be, into the development of this theme. The section culminates in a survey of about twenty five examples of modern research work in biology.[98]

Above Jacqueline's three-dimensional screen for *The Living World* section of the *Dome of Discovery* at the Festival of Britain on the South Bank, 1951.

Opposite Misha Black under the *Dome of Discovery!* One of a series of images by Clifford Hatts, for Black's own use as Christmas cards, 1951. Courtesy of Clifford Hatts

[96] *The Catalogue of Exhibits, South Bank Exhibition, The Festival of Britain 1951*, HMSO, p.88.

[97] Ibid. p.111.

[98] Ibid.

[99] AAD.

[100] Ibid, information written on reverse of press photograph.

[101] Prokop, pp.125-128.

[102] John T. Murray, 'The Cheap Need Not Be Cheap And Nasty', *Design*, December 1950.

[103] Geoffrey Rayner, Richard Chamberlain and Annamarie Stapleton, *Artist Textiles in Britain, 1945-1970*, Antique Collectors' Club, 2003, p.82.

Working under the umbrella of the DRU, Jacqueline's task was to create a large scale three-dimensional sculptural screen as an imposing entrance to *The Living World*. The form of this remarkable screen was that of a large squared up abacus, strung with organic sculptural components which were based on 'natural forms' and casts from naturally occurring found objects such as 'mussel shells and eccentrically shaped stones'.[99] Decorations derived from molecular imagery were rife at the Festival and in each of the screen's large elements, smaller individual components were strung and suspended to appear like free-floating molecules contained within a grid-like frame, strongly reminiscent of Josef Hoffmann's early work. To achieve this Jacqueline first constructed a large single element which she repeated thirty times, in three rows of ten – essentially the same method she used for building up two-dimensional designs from collaged PMTs of a single image.

Jacqueline translated the organic molecular imagery of her screen for *The Living World* exhibit into a textile design for another project for the Festival, which was much closer to her heart. In England Jacques had received few, if any, substantial commissions for public architectural or interior design projects. This situation was somewhat redressed when the Council of Industrial Design gave Jacques the commission to design the Festival's Information Centre and West End office, situated in the Swan and Edgar department store in London's Regent Street. Although small in scale and away from the main Festival site, Jacques, with Jacqueline, made it an impressive assignment: the final sparks from the embers of their shared Secessionist inheritance of the Gesamtkunstwerk. Jacques brought all his ability and experience to resolve the problems of the difficult space given to house the Centre, for which he created a bright and vibrant modern environment. He also either designed or selected the furnishings and fittings, most memorable of which was the intelligent and elegant design of the long asymmetrical information desk, realised in mahogany, and the equally elegant chairs he chose to complement it, designed by Dennis Lennon for the Scottish Furniture Manufacturers.[100]

Jacqueline created colour schemes for Jacques' designs. For the waiting room she selected shades of gold and for the Information Centre deep green and vermilion. She also designed a textile for the decorative wall panelling in green and gold with a large scale pattern, clearly derived from the organic sculptural forms of her screen for *The Living World* exhibit. The textile was given a successful afterlife in 1952, when Jacqueline redesigned a more decorative version on a smaller domestic scale for commercial production by David Whitehead, a progressive and innovative company with an avowedly popularist approach to good design. Like the version of her earlier textile for the Rayon Design Centre, also produced by Whitehead, this version of the Information Centre textile has since become synonymous with the 1950s and at the time won many friends in the trade press through its extreme economy of form and bold elegance.[101]

Another outstanding example of Jacqueline's pattern design, a wallpaper, was chosen for the *Hobbies And The Home* section of the Festival's *House and Gardens Pavilion*. Both the design and the selection of the furnishings and fittings for the various room-sets in the section were the work of the brothers, artists and textile designers, Roger and Robert Nicholson. Roger was later Professor of Textile Design at the Royal College of Art from 1958 to 1984. The wallpaper manufacturer John Line and

Co had commissioned a portfolio of hand-screen-printed modern designs, *The Limited Editions Collection*, expressly for display at the Festival. The collection was designed by leading artists and designers, amongst whom were Jacqueline, Lucienne Day and the painter John Minton. Jacqueline's nursery wallpaper, *Kiddies Town*, was chosen by the Nicholsons for use in the Play Room exhibit. The vitality of the design owes something to the work of the painter Paul Klee, who Jacqueline acknowledged as one of the two greatest influences on her work. She designed children's wallpapers and fabrics throughout her career and their design was one of the projects she regularly set her students.

Jacqueline's redesign of her Rayon Design Centre textile for David Whitehead was included in the group of twenty textiles chosen for the company's display at the Festival. Her textiles were shown alongside others by Roger Nicholson and a young Terence Conran, who was then Dennis Lennon's assistant at the Rayon Design Centre. A key contact at Whiteheads was the architect John T. Murray. Murray had been appointed Director of Furnishing Fabrics for David Whitehead in 1948, as part of a plan to make the company a market leader in the manufacture of modern textiles. He had an agenda for achieving this, which he clearly laid out in 'The Cheap Need Not Be Cheap And Nasty' in the Council of Industrial Design's magazine, *Design*, December 1950:

It is true that a certain amount of lip service is paid to good design, but the instances in which an ostensible belief is carried into commercial practice are very few, moreover much of the good design which is produced is confined to the higher price ranges, catering for the statistically insignificant wealthy class. My own firm, on the other hand, caters for those vast sections of humanity in which the emphasis is on cheapness and serviceability … The process of making money and making fine things are not mutually exclusive.[102]

Apart from the quality of their manufacture, Whitehead textiles were exceptional for the quality of their design, commissioned from leading avant-garde artists and designers. Amongst these were Henry Moore, John Piper, Eduardo Paolozzi, Terence Conran and Jacqueline. Having created a winning formula for Whitehead, John Murray left at the height of the company's success in 1952 and was succeeded the following year by the architect Tom Mellor. Jacqueline continued as a freelance designer for Whitehead until at least 1954. One of her textiles for the company at this time again reflects the influence of her *Living World* screen.

For another manufacturer, Haworth Fabrics, Jacqueline continued the organic sculptural theme she had developed for the Festival of Britain, with a design for a textile, circa 1952, of a collage of organic forms strung and suspended on a line, very like Paolozzi's sculpture of the late 1940s. A photograph of two other textiles for Haworth Fabrics is in the Groag archive, the National Archive of Art and Design, and a colour slide of one of these, annotated 'Haworth Fabrics, 1953', is also held in the Design Council's archive, the University of Brighton. All three textiles are printed on a very distinctive spun rayon, quite different in its weave from that used by David Whitehead, with which they might otherwise be confused.

John Murray's reference to good design for the wealthy class was probably referring to the textiles of Edinburgh Weavers, who, besides Whitehead, was the other most progressive textile manufacturer in Britain. Edinburgh Weavers was the 'baby' of Alastair Morton, a member of the Morton dynasty, proprietors of the distinguished Scottish textile manufacturer Morton Sundour. Edinburgh Weavers had been set up in 1928 by Alastair's father, James Morton, as an experimental unit for researching the relationship between modern art and the design and production of textiles suitable for use in contemporary architectural settings. The running of the company was taken over by Alastair in 1932. He was himself a Constructivist painter, as well as designer and weaver, and his deep interest and commitment to modern art and design led him, over the next thirty years, to take Edinburgh Weavers to an extreme position in the production of Modernist textiles.

Unlike the inexpensive mass market that Whitehead's textiles were intended for, the textiles of Edinburgh Weavers were aimed at the elite world of architects and interior designers. Many had originally been commissioned for particular projects and were only subsequently available for general sale. The woven textile *Avon*, for example, was designed by the painter Cecil Collins and commissioned by the Ministry of Works in 1960 for use in the new conference hall in the British Embassy in Washington; each individual pattern repeat was a little over fifteen feet (four and a half metres).[103]

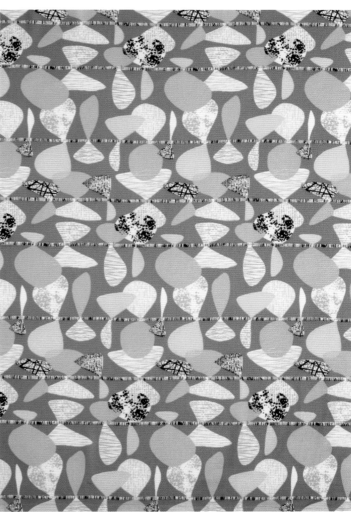

Opposite After the Festival David Whitehead produced a commercial version of Jacqueline's textile for the Information Centre on roller-printed rayon. It proved very popular with the public. Collection H. Kirk Brown III and Jill A. Wiltse

Opposite inset The Festival of Britain Information Centre at Swan & Edgar's department store, London, designed by Jacques Groag, with textiles designed Jacqueline and printed by the Calico Printers Association.

Above left The artwork for *Kiddies Town*, a wallpaper produced by John Line, 1951, in red on a white ground and exhibited at the Festival of Britain. *Kiddies Town* shows Jacqueline's debt to Paul Klee and illustrates Reilly's comments that in her design repertoire Jacqueline 'brings back the freshness and outlook of a child'. Collection H. Kirk Brown III and Jill A. Wiltse

Above right Textile showing the influence of Jacqueline's screen for the Dome of Discovery at the Festival of Britain. Roller-printed on a spun rayon fabric distinctive of that used by Haworth Fabrics, circa 1953. Collection H. Kirk Brown III and Jill A. Wiltse

On a typewritten label on the reverse of a PMT of the finished artwork for another textile by Jacqueline is the information 'Design for a furnishing textile for the Edinburgh Weavers, designed 1956. The textile was available on the market by the spring of 1957'.[104] An original collage for the same design, now in a private collection, is annotated 'Design for the Edinburgh Weavers, 1957', but with no indication if it was woven or printed.[105] Another by Jacqueline for Edinburgh Weavers, *Xanadu*, a woven textile from 1955, is better documented and is illustrated in the *Studio Year Book* for 1956.

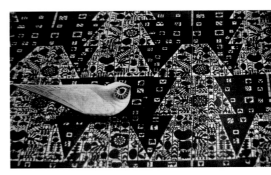

A woven textile from the early 1950s attributed to Jacqueline is closely related to her screen for *The Living World* exhibit at The Festival of Britain. It is even more striking in its relationship to her textile for the Festival Information Centre, as is the peacock blue green of the background and golden yellow of the pattern. The complexity, subtlety and richness of the weave indicates it being a product of Edinburgh Weavers, but, surprisingly, considering it is an outstanding textile of such high quality, it does not appear to have been reproduced in any contemporary publication. It was probably a commission of Jacqueline's for a particular client and produced for them by Edinburgh Weavers.

Jacqueline's success at the Festival and the exposure of her work in *The Ambassador* probably contributed to the revival of interest first shown in her work in America in the 1930s. From 1952 she began to develop successful working relationships with a number of American companies which were to last throughout the 1950s and into the 1960s. Her re-emergence on the American design scene was announced by her design for the cover of the February 1953 issue of the American magazine *Interiors*. A note inside the cover records it being based on a design from a portfolio of wallpaper patterns she brought to the USA in late 1952. From this it seems she had recommenced her pre-war practice of travelling abroad seeking new clients. She must have already visited the US before the end of 1952, however, as her first textile for Associated American Artists, *Good Morning!*, had been released for sale earlier that year and was one of the first, if not the first, in the Associated American Artists range of textiles.

Associated American Artists (AAA), an altruistic venture with its origins in the Depression, was founded in 1934 with the aim of making fine art affordable and easily accessible to all. This was initially achieved by selling large

Above right *Xanadu*, a jacquard woven textile for Edinburgh Weavers, 1955. Private Collection.

Bottom right Artwork for *Herba Benedicta*, a printed cotton furnishing textile for Edinburgh Weavers dated 1957. Collection H. Kirk Brown III and Jill A. Wiltse.

Opposite Cover for the American magazine *Interiors,* published February 1953.

[104] AAD.

[105] H Kirk Brown III Collection.

[106] Karen Herbaugh, conference paper, 'The Associated American Artists: Textile Art For The Masses', The Textile Society of America, 8th Biennial Symposium, Smith College Campus, Northampton, Massachusetts, 26-28 September 2002.

[107] Ibid.

[108] AAD.

[109] HKB III Coll.

[110] Ibid.

[111] AAD.

editions of signed original artists' lithographs and etchings through some fifty department stores. In the early 1950s AAA also began commissioning designs for furnishing and fashion fabrics from American artists, illustrators and graphic designers. Karen Herbaugh writes that:

These fabrics, which are titled, signed, and dated on the selvage, were heralded at their introduction by newspaper articles, shelter and apparel magazines – both for the public and trade. Macy's department store was integral in the promotion of the early fabrics, creating vignettes throughout the store to introduce each fabric line.[106]

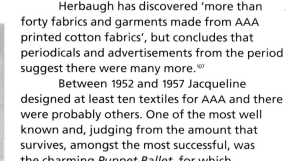

Herbaugh has discovered 'more than forty fabrics and garments made from AAA printed cotton fabrics', but concludes that periodicals and advertisements from the period suggest there were many more.[107]

Between 1952 and 1957 Jacqueline designed at least ten textiles for AAA and there were probably others. One of the most well known and, judging from the amount that survives, amongst the most successful, was the charming *Puppet Ballet*, for which Jacqueline once again breathed life into her dolls. The witty *Family Outing* is a design of colourful birds placed against a classic Hoffmann grid which clearly shows her Werkstätte inheritance. As always, she successfully translated her training with Hoffmann and her Viennese background into the current idiom of her host country, creating for AAA a vibrant and essentially 'American Modern' style.

The news of the success of her cover design for *Interiors* and her textile designs for AAA appears to have quickly spread and Jacqueline soon acquired an American client group. She listed a number of American textile manufacturers she worked for[108] although most are no more than a name on the reverse of a textile design. Amongst these is a design for a company named Reeves and another for Heyter, New York; both date from the 1950s. A third New York textile manufacturer she designed for was Delsey Fabrics; the artwork for two variations of a design for this company, now in a private collection, is dated 1958.[109] An advertisement for the Isabel Scott Fabrics Corp, New York, around 1955, uses three dress fabrics by Jacqueline, the artwork for one of which, *Everyday Humor*, also survives.[110] One other design from the 1950s, *Cleo*, Jacqueline also recorded as sold to the US,[111] and a dress fabric with a variation of her Wiener Werkstätte influenced 'tulip' pattern is American in origin. There is no indication who these last two designs were for and much more research is yet to be done on her work in America.

This Jacquard woven
furnishing fabric, attributed
to Edinburgh Weavers,
is closely related to
Jacqueline's textile for the
Festival of Britain Information
Centre and her *Living World*
screen for the *Dome of
Discovery*. Collection H. Kirk
Brown III and Jill A. Wiltse.

Good Morning!, printed
cotton dress fabric
produced by Associated
American Artists, 1952.
Collection H. Kirk Brown III
and Jill A. Wiltse

Puppet Ballet, 1953.
Printed cotton dress fabric,
produced by Associated
American Artists.
Private collection

Family Outing, printed
cotton dress fabric
produced by Associated
American Artists, 1954.
Collection H. Kirk Brown III
and Jill A. Wiltse

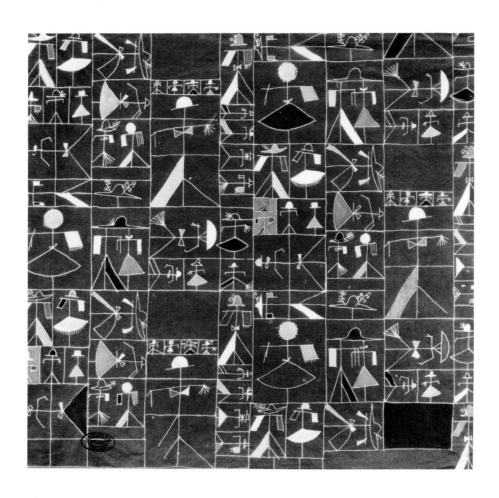

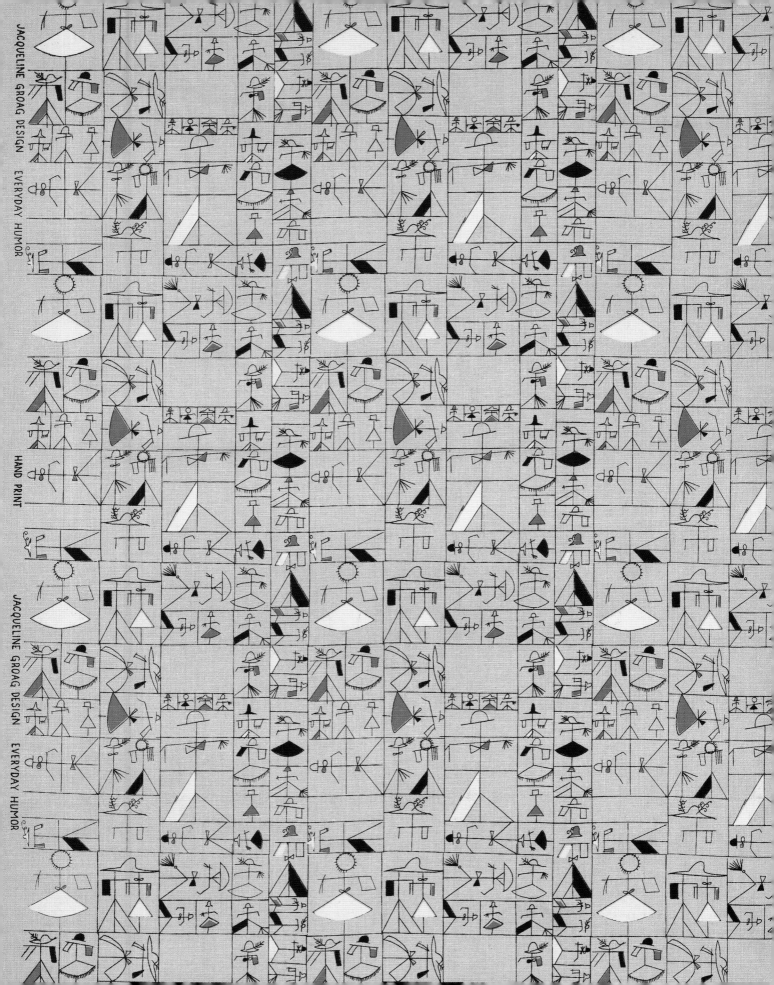

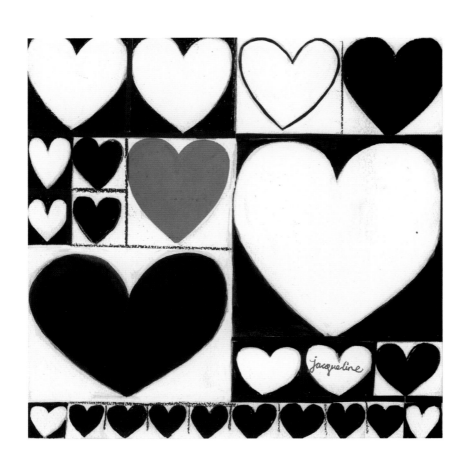

Artwork for a Valentine's Day
card, probably for Hallmark
Cards Inc, New York, early
1960s. Collection H. Kirk
Brown III and Jill A. Wiltse.

Christmas card designed by
Jacqueline for the Architects'
Benevolent Fund, circa 1962.
Collection Alison Musker

Although Jacqueline had designed wrapping paper and stationery previously, a new departure was the design of greetings cards in the late 1950s and 1960s for American Greetings, Ohio, and Hallmark Cards Inc, New York. Artworks for two Valentine cards from the early 1960s were probably for Hallmark[112] and she was particularly pleased to have persuaded Hallmark to introduce her Christmas card designs using modern images of Madonnas and angels.[113] About this time she also designed cards for James Valentine and Sons, Dundee, Scotland. It was probably following Jacques' death in 1962 that she designed, possibly as a gift, Christmas cards for the Architects' Benevolent Fund and, a little later, dual-purpose Christmas cards/decorations in embossed gold card for Oxfam-Unicef.[114] The Victoria and Albert Museum's Department of Prints and Drawings also holds the artwork for what appears to be a gift-wrapping paper for the British Overseas Airways Corporation (BOAC).[115] Following her cover designs for *The Ambassador* in the late 1940s and designs for menus and so on for Kardomah in 1950, graphic design became an increasing part of Jacqueline's work. For example, she recorded gift items she had designed for Liberty of London in the early 1960s, such as decorated books of matches,[116] as well as textiles.

1957-1962:
Trains and Boats and Planes

For the design of the *63* range of playing cards and packaging for The De La Rue Company, Jacqueline won the highest award in the *Sports Goods and Recreational Equipment* section of the 1963 *Starpacks* competition.[117] At that time De La Rue was the major shareholder of the American plastic laminate manufacturer, Formica. Plastic laminates decorated with marble and wood grain effects had been around since the late 1920s, but it was not until after the Second World War that strongly patterned and fully heat-resistant decorative laminates were developed suitable for use in domestic interiors. An early example dated 1946 for Warerite, with a design by the sculptor Henry Moore, exists in the Ascher Archive. This was used for the tops of the *BC* tables designed by Ernest Race and used in the Tea Bar of *Britain Can Make It*.[118] Charles Reilly's son, Paul, writes that,

Already before the war British Warerite boards had been produced incorporating original designs for decorative murals; the artists had worked direct on to specially prepared paper which was then incorporated in the top surface of the laminate.[119]

Jacqueline later created large laminated decorative panels using this method, but her first designs for laminates seem to have been for De La Rue in 1954. Although De la Rue were not the majority shareholders of Formica until 1958, they held distribution rights for the company's laminates in Europe, and a number of laminates for Formica by the De La Rue Design Group were published in *Design*, December 1954. At least one, *Cocktail*, and probably a second, are in Jacqueline's distinctive hand. De La Rue rarely credited individual designers and no particular name is associated with any of the designs.[120]

In the early 1950s plastics were the new wonder materials in the home; they represented modernity and the future and most companies and corporations wanted a piece of the action. The giant chemicals company ICI was no exception. It had already developed, in the 1930s, but not commercially exploited until the early 1950s, a protein fibre cloth, *Ardil,* suitable for a variety of domestic uses. Robin Day was engaged to design a range of publicity material for the product in 1952[121] and in 1953 the company commissioned Jacqueline to create suitable designs. *Ardil* cloth was printed by Liberty of London at their Langley Printworks. The Liberty archive holds the artwork for two of Jacqueline's designs for *Ardil*, another is in the Groag Archive and two closely related artworks are in a private collection. Around this time she also made designs for another plastic cloth, a type of soft plastic sheeting produced by a German company, Göppinger Kaliko und Kunstlerderwerke.[122]

Although her principal activity remained textile design, as the 1950s progressed Jacqueline became increasingly involved with the design of plastic laminates, often expressly for use in the interiors of major public transport projects. The Austrian émigré designer, Gaby Schreiber, was commissioned in 1958 by BOAC to oversee all aspects of design for their aircraft interiors. The commission may have originally come through Misha Black and the Design Research Unit. As a young man, the former head of BBC television set design, Clifford Hatts, had been a member of the DRU team working under Black's direction on the exhibition design and displays in the *Dome of Discovery* at the Festival of Britain. He recalls he had been aware at various times of Gaby Schreiber and Jacqueline as Associate Designers of the DRU. The organisation had a small flexible core of full time designers who, when necessary, were augmented by freelance designers brought in to work on particular commissions.[123]

Above right and centre
Laminated playing cards and packaging for De La Rue, 1963.

Below right *Cocktail,* a plastic laminate attributed to Jacqueline, designed for the De La Rue Design Group and produced by Formica, 1954.

[112] HKB III Coll.

[113] Anscombe/Groag.

[114] HKB III Coll.

[115] DPP.

[116] Fiona MacCarthy and Patrick Nuttgens, *Eye For Industry: Royal Designers for Industry, 1936-1986,* Lund Humphries, in association with the Royal Society of Arts, London 1986, p.93.

[117] *Design* No 170 February 1963, p.62.

[118] *Britain Can Make It* (BCMI) Exhibition Catalogue, Council of Industrial Design, HMSO, 1946, pp.46. The catalogue lists these tables as having, 'tops made from a plastic print by Warerite Ltd, of a design by Ascher Fabrics Ltd.' A small sample of this laminate, the design by Henry Moore, remains in the Ascher Archive.

[119] Paul Reilly, 'A Decorative Future For Plastic Laminates', *Design,* December 1954, no 72, pp.9-13.

[120] Ibid.

[121] *Art & Industry,* May 1952, p.158.

[122] AAD.

[123] Clifford Hatts, interview with the authors, November 2008.

[124] June Lyons, interview with the authors, 2001.

[125] Hugh Sutherland, 'Design For Jet-Travel, Design for Industry', *Studio* Ltd, p.21, no. 393, vol. 66, March 1959. Other related information in Groag Archive, AAD.

[126] HKB III Coll.

[127] AAD.

[128] Ibid.

[129] Ibid.

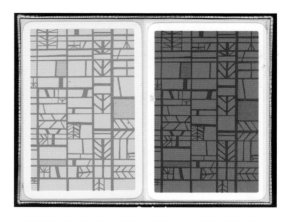

An example of this is when the architect Frederick Gibberd commissioned DRU to carry out the interior design of his new buildings for Heathrow Airport in the mid-1950s. DRU engaged the pattern designer June Lyons, as an Associate, to design the textiles and wallpapers for the project.[124] This was normal practice; other design teams worked on the same basis and could in turn take on full responsibility for the overall design, co-ordination and management of a project on behalf of DRU. Specialist designers, such as Jacqueline, would be appointed Associates for specific tasks.

Schreiber commissioned Jacqueline to create patterns for multiple uses within the interiors of BOAC's Boeing 707s and de Havilland Comet 4s. Her designs, such as *Grasses,* were used not only for seat covers, but also for decorative wall panels made from Synthede, and a polyvinyl upholstery cloth called 'Lionide', both produced by Jas. Williamson and Son.[125] On the original artwork of another design for this commission, of small delicate botanical studies, now in a private collection, Jacqueline has written of her inspiration for the design and suggestions for its realisation,

Gowing Up
Inside aircrafts to remind passengers on good old earth and flowers.
Can be done visa-versa black lettering on ivory backgrounds. Or in 2 greens only on ivory ground.
I'd suggest to print it in this tiny size, easy to use – anywhere.[126]

As an Associate of DRU Jacqueline also designed patterns for plastic laminates for panelling, tables and bar tops for British Rail. In 1960 she created decorative wall panels for British Rail's *Silver Train*.[127] Laminated panels had been used for the decoration of ships since before the Second World War. For such panels. Jacqueline developed her own method of decoration: she first hand-silkscreened the design on to the panel, which she then worked with hand-colouring and a sgraffito technique she termed hand-engraving. These panels were widely used by British Rail on their trains in the 1960s. There is also a record of her designing for BEA coaches, probably a commission from Gaby Schreiber.[128]

Jacqueline was commissioned in about 1960 by the architect Neville Ward – recalled by Clifford Hatts as a name he remembers associated with DRU – to make designs for the interiors of the cargo and ocean steamships of the A.H. Holt Shipping Co. As part of the commission she created five large decorative panels, for use in the Masters' and Captains' day rooms on the cargo boats.[129] These were reliefs for which she used large metal sheets she had covered with plaster of Paris, which she then

USE IN:

INSIDE
AIRCRAFTS
TO REMIND
PASSENGERS
ON GOOD
OLD EARTH
AND
FLOWERS.

„GOWING UP.."

CAN BE DONE   VISA — VERSA.
BLACK LEAVES ON   IVORY

BACKGROUNDS.

OR in 2   greens  only
on ivory ground.

I'D SUGGEST TO PRINT
IT IN THIS TINY SIZE!

EASY TO USE = ANYWHERE.

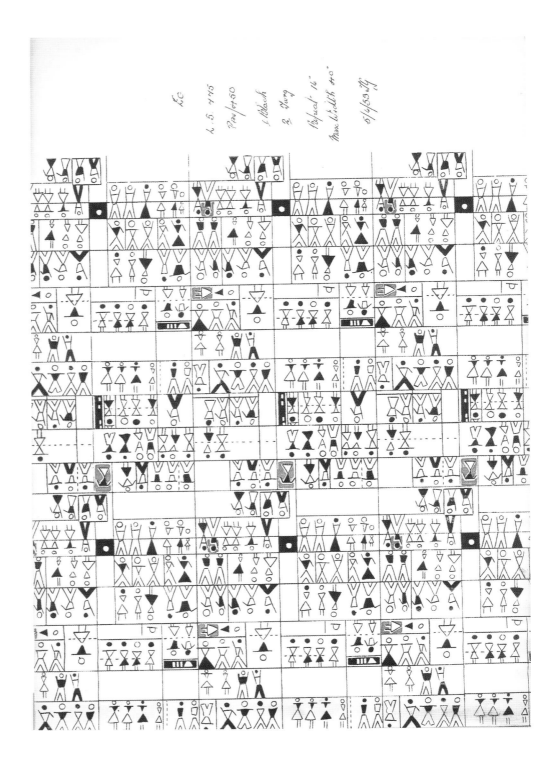

Left 'Gowing Up', a design sheet for BOAC, 1959. Collection H. Kirk Brown III and Jill A. Wiltse

Right Paper strike-off for one of Jacqueline's designs intended to be printed on *Ardil*, a man-made fibre. *Ardil* was developed by ICI and printed at Liberty of London's Merton Abbey or Langley Printworks.

inscribed, carved and sgrafittoed and painted white. Jacqueline's records also show another shipping company she worked for, The British Holland and Channel Line, although she gives no other information.[130]

From the late 1950s to the early 1960s the design of plastic laminates became an increasing part of Jacqueline's work. As well as those for particular commissions, such as that for British Rail, she also designed commercial ranges for Warerite, Harrison and Sons and the Swedish company, Perstorp, who later merged with Warerite. The range for Warerite was particularly successful and included the well-known and popular designs *Alexandretta* and *Lilliput*. Her extensive range for Harrison and Sons was released for sale in 1963.[131] During the early 1960s Jacqueline's work became less focused and, other than that for John Lewis, consisted of fewer commissions from a much more varied client group.

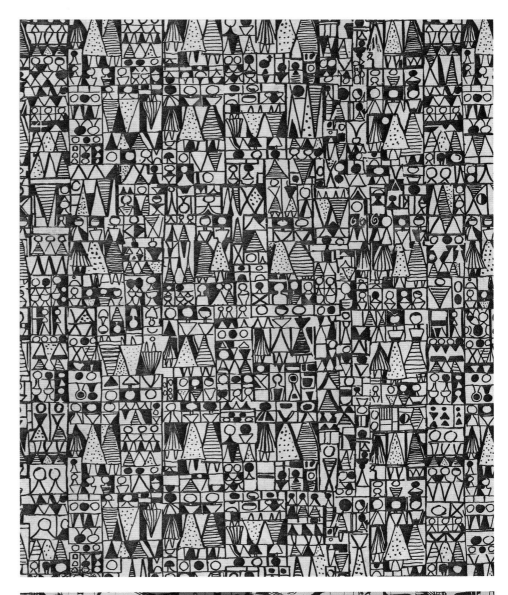

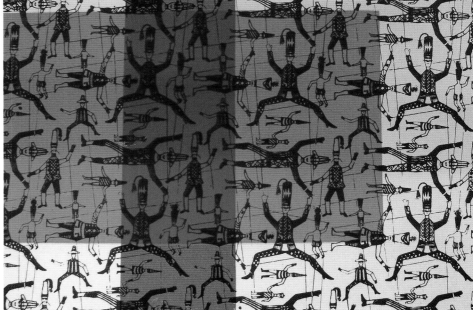

Opposite Artwork for *Alexandretta,* a laminate design for Warerite which relies on her naive child-like drawing and is based on her doll collection. Collection H. Kirk Brown III and Jill A. Wiltse.

Top right Artwork for *Lilliput,* a small scale design for a laminate produced by Warerite in 1960 and later by Harrison & Sons as *Parade.* Collection H. Kirk Brown III and Jill A. Wiltse.

Below right Harrison & Sons sales brochure, circa 1962, illustrating Jacqueline's *Jumping Jacks* design.

130 Ibid.

131 Ibid.

One obvious and sad reason for this hiatus in Jacqueline's work was Jacques' death in 1962. It was an occasion for many obituaries and tributes, in particular the memorial lecture by Stefan Buzas. Jacqueline's grief can well be imagined. For thirty-two years they had lived in an almost symbiotic union as Jacqueline and Jacques. Professionally, emotionally, artistically, intellectually and – as Jacqueline would have expressed it – spiritually, they had been the creative mainspring of each others' lives. There is little evidence, if any, in either the Groag Archive, or the reminiscences of friends and acquaintances, of how Jacqueline coped with her loss, or the effect it had on her work in the long term.

By the late 1950s she was becoming increasingly dependent on Misha Black and Gaby Schreiber for major commissions. Such commissions were essential if she was to maintain a high profile for her work with other professionals and attract potential clients. Like Jacqueline, both Misha and Gaby were Jewish émigrés. Misha had been brought from Russia to Britain by his parents as a two year old, but Gaby had arrived as a young adult from Vienna in 1939. From 1949, when he first commissioned Jacqueline to work on the Kardomah tea shops and coffee houses, Misha became one of her principal supporters and patrons. Photographs exist of a further DRU project, for Dunlop, which Jacqueline worked on as an Associate Designer.[132] She also recorded on the list of companies she had worked for the name of Standard Telephone and Cable, London, probably another DRU project.[133] With their similar backgrounds, competing in what could be a misogynistic, xenophobic and anti-Semitic workplace, Gaby and Jacqueline would have shared a mutual empathy, which may have been influential in Gaby's decision to give Jacqueline the BOAC commission.

With the closure of the Festival of Britain, although commissions from Misha and Gaby and her work in America, particularly for Associated American Artists, continued, there was a slow falling away of Jacqueline's career. This was more so after Jacques' death. The John Lewis Partnership was the one client for whom she worked consistently, until well into the 1970s. The success of her commercial ranges of plastic laminates for Warerite and Harrison in the 1960s would have been a spin-off of her widely publicised work for Misha and Gaby. She did one later range of laminates for Warerite which

was launched in the summer of 1969,[134] some of which were included in the Design Index of the Council of Industrial Design, a recognition of her contribution to the British design industry.

Another old acquaintance key to Jacqueline's work at this time was her loyal friend and client John Murray, the design consultant for Warerite from the late 1950s and into the 1960s. He had successfully commissioned textile designs from her for Whitehead and after leaving the company in 1952 had remained in contact. Following his departure from Whitehead he was appointed Director of Design for the carpet manufacturer Bond Worth and in 1957 he commissioned eight designs from Jacqueline for the *Acropolis* range. These carpets were marketed in tandem with the *Spectrum* range of woven textiles, produced by Prospect Manufacturing Co, another firm under Murray's direction. The following year, 1958, Bond Worth launched a further six designs by Jacqueline as the *Augustine* range. Murray commissioned them to be a more competitively priced range than the *Acropolis*, but with no change in the quality of their design, in true Whitehead style.[135] Jacqueline's last known designs for carpets were for the manufacturer Andrew Gaskell in about 1967. An article in *Design*, 1968, reported she had been given complete freedom in order to achieve the end product.[136]

The Wallpaper Manufacturers (WPM) launched, in 1960, amid much publicity, their prestigious *Modus* range of wallpapers. These were chiefly aimed at architects and interior designers and the range included designs by Terence Conran, Lucienne Day, the artist William Gear, and two designs by Jacqueline, *Adagio* and *Precious Stones*.[137] Her last known designs for wallpapers were executed in 1976 for the Finnish company Sandudd Vantaa. Although

Right Design for a tulip patterned carpet for Bond-Worth, circa 1957.

Opposite Six of Jacqueline's eight designs for the carpet manufacturer Bond Worth's *Acropolis* range, 1957.

[132] Ibid.

[133] Ibid.

[134] *Design*, no 247, July 1969, p.68.

[135] *House and Garden*, Condé Nast Publications Ltd, September 1958, pp.22-25. Further information for the *Acropolis* range is in the Groag Archive, AAD.

[136] *Design*, no 238, October 1968, p.75.

[137] *Design*, no 144, December 1960, p.1. *Design*, no. 150, June1 1961, back cover.

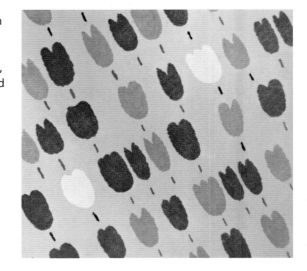

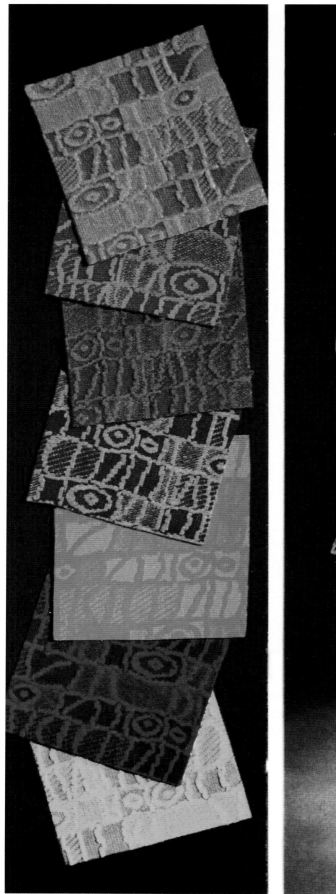

Jacqueline had continuously engaged with new materials and technology, one new departure for her as a textile designer was a commission she received in about 1966 from Charnos for a new ICI developed textile, Crimplene. Charnos considered it a 'wonder' material and the 'most versatile manmade fabric yet'. Jacqueline's design, *Mosaic*, was strongly influenced by psychedelia and was available in twenty-four different luminous colourways.[138]

During the 1970s she worked on a number of exciting projects for DRU, and a final group of textiles for the John Lewis Partnership. In 1975 she designed a wall covering for Sealink ferries, a subsidiary of British Rail, for which she used, once more, a version of her Werkstätte-inspired tulip design.[139] For her designs for London Transport[140] she returned to yet another classic Viennese motif: a Josef Hoffmann-inspired grid pattern. This project was co-ordinated by Misha Black for DRU and resulted in one of the best-known upholstery textiles for London's buses and tubes in the 1970s. Towards the end of the 1970s she received a commission from the Italian chemicals company Monsanto for wall coverings for an exhibition pavilion.[141] This, her last commission for textiles for a particular situation, brought her full circle: working alongside an architect and other designers in an example of the Gesamtkunstwerk, the ideal of the Vienna Secession.

By the mid-1960s Jacqueline had developed a further string to her bow and began teaching. In the early 1980s she made a list of the twenty-five pupils, for whom she used her 'own teaching method', something she emphasised.[142] Her method would have

Opposite Magazine advertisement for ICI's Crimplene fabric using Jacqueline's design, *Mosaic*, 1967.

Above Furnishing textile designed by Jacqueline Groag circa 1968.

Right Design for nursery wallpaper, 1971. Gouache on paper. Executed by Alison Musker whilst studying with Jacqueline. Courtesy of Alison Musker

138 *The Ambassador,* No 2 1967, p.51.

139 A design for wall covering for Sealink, 1975, DPP.

140 AAD.

141 Photograph in the Groag Archive, AAD.

142 AAD.

owed much to the teaching of the Kunstgewerbeschule, and Josef Hoffmann and Franz Cizek. A typewritten paper exists describing her curriculum and giving the terms of enrolment and fees for the course:

Enrolment is made on a selective basis after two tentative private lessons at 3 Guineas each 2 hour session.

One course consisting of ten private sessions – 30 guineas.

Fees should be paid in advance: fair notice should be given in case of cancellations.

After completion of design course students will be given further guidance and advice with regard to establishing contact with prospective clients and starting a free-lance practice.[143]

In the case of one student, the artist Alison Musker, 'enrolment … made on a selective basis' is an extreme understatement. Alison moved in court circles and a friend of hers was Sir David Checketts. After serving as Equerry to the Duke of Edinburgh, Sir David had been appointed Equerry to the future Prince of Wales in 1967, and subsequently became the Prince's Private Secretary and Treasurer of the Prince's Household. Whilst attending a dinner party at Sir David's home in 1971, Alison mentioned that, having studied painting, she would like to take a course in design, but had no idea how to start. Sir David suggested the Duke of Edinburgh might have some ideas and, as he was expecting a 'phone call from the Duke that very evening, he would raise the matter with him whilst Alison was there. When Sir David returned from his conversation with the Duke, he told Alison the Duke was willing to help and even had someone in mind who might be suitable as a teacher. The Duke suggested Alison first attempt a number of designs and bring the result to the Palace, for him to look them over. She did so, and the Duke obviously thought her work up to scratch, for Alison next received a letter inviting her to visit Jacqueline at her studio in Clifton Hill, London.

However, it was only after Alison had taken the two required preliminary lessons that Jacqueline finally accepted her as a student. In the event, Alison was unable to complete the full course of ten lessons, although she found Jacqueline personally delightful and her teaching all absorbing. She was so entranced by the entire experience that she failed to register much of the house and studio, other than its simple white minimalism. Jacqueline was not in the habit of allowing visitors access to her studio and any ongoing work was removed when she used it for teaching. This, in theory, did not allow her students to be unnecessarily influenced by her. In Alison's case however,

Jacqueline's special teaching methods proved extraordinarily effective, for examples of Alison's design work, done under Jacqueline's tuition, can well be mistaken for Jacqueline's own work. One of the exercises Jacqueline set Alison was to design a children's wallpaper, a favourite subject of hers. Alison's is extremely close in style to Jacqueline's. Considering the short time Alison studied with Jacqueline she achieved a fair amount of work, the result, as she puts it, of 'lots of Prep'. Even now, after so many years, Alison continues to hold Jacqueline in great respect and on her curriculum vitae claims her, with some pride, as her teacher.[144]

The remarkable circumstances of Alison Musker's introduction to Jacqueline by the Duke of Edinburgh possibly resulted from a knowledge the Duke had of Jacqueline's work going back to the 1940s. It is often forgotten that, like Prince Albert previously, the Duke has long taken a special interest in design; in the 1950s 'The Duke of Edinburgh's Award for Elegant Design', was given annually by the Council of Industrial Design. Jacqueline's tulip textile used in 1946 for the widely publicised dress by Edward Molyneux for the Queen when Princess Elizabeth, may well have first brought Jacqueline's work to the Duke's attention. Alison says it is known that the Duke has always taken an interest in the Queen's fashions. Whatever the reason, the Duke was certainly aware of Jacqueline's teaching activities, even possibly her financial situation, and showed her consideration and respect by carefully vetting Alison and her work before putting her in touch with Jacqueline.

In the mid-1950s Jacques and Jacqueline moved to their final home together, 26 Clifton Hill. It is a classic semi-detached Regency Villa, which had then been recently refurbished by Sigmund Freud's son, the architect Ernst Freud. The adjoining house, number 28, had also been refurbished by Ernst and lived in, for a while, by his son, the painter Lucien Freud. By the time Jacques and Jacqueline moved into 26, number 28 was occupied by Lucien Freud's cousin, Sigmund Freud's great nephew by marriage: Richard Mosse. One of Richard's sons, James, remembers Jacques and Jacqueline well. He recalls Jacques as a bad tempered old man, who was touchy, irritable and not fond of children. Jacques was forever complaining about any noise James and his siblings made when playing in the garden, even writing to James' father to complain of the children running up and down the steps from the house into the garden, as they could be observed by burglars

143 Ibid.

144 Alison Musker, interviews with the authors, June/July 2008.

145 James Mosse, interviews with the authors, November 2008.

146 Cox.

147 Anscombe/Groag.

148 Irvine.

149 Timmers.

150 Isabelle Anscombe, *A Woman's Touch, Women in Design from 1860 to the Present Day,* pp.113, 193-194.

151 AAD.

who would then know the way into the houses![145] Susan Cox had written in 1945 that Jacques' inability to tolerate noise was the reason Jacqueline had not taken the apartment in Albany Terrace as a home. James Mosse also remembers the very marked tremor of Jacques' hands, something others, such as Kate Irvine, have commented on, and of which Jacqueline was not very patient. Both Jacques' intolerance of noise and the tremor of his hands were probably legacies of a mental breakdown in the early 1940s, when Susan Cox described Jacques as ' … having been very ill and is now very nervy'.[146]

James Mosse remembers Jacqueline in the 1960s appearing somewhat sweet, innocent and naive, and, although in her sixties, incongruously giving the impression of being a young girl of fourteen or fifteen. Although very young himself at the time, he somehow sensed this to be an affectation and a contrived stance on the part of an extremely sophisticated adult. In an interview in 1981, Jacqueline not only claimed to have an inner age of eight, but that, although approaching eighty, the majority of her friends were then under thirty.[147] One young man who became a friend of Jacqueline later in her life was a tenant of James' father, and Kate Irvine recalled another young man, a Chinese professional pianist, who was also a close friend in her final years.[148]

James and his wife, the academic and writer Lesley Hoskins, particularly remember how Jacqueline, in the mid-1970s, with her bobbed ash blond hair and wearing a full-length white leather coat, could have passed from behind for a fashionable young woman. However, like Elsbeth Juda, James says Jacqueline was not fashionable in a superficially conventional way, but had an innate elegance and sense of style, which always seemed exactly right. In the 1960s and 1970s Jacqueline's style was enhanced by the clothes of the radical American fashion designer, Bonnie Cashin, who then had a boutique in Liberty of London. According to James, Jacqueline never wore flowing or loose clothes, or A-line dresses. Her clothes were always cut straight and without fuss, and were usually made in leather, mohair, cashmere or jersey wool, mainly in shades of white or, occasionally, black, very much the Cashin style.

Another who came to know Jacqueline well in her final years was Margaret Timmers, a curator in the Victoria and Albert Museum's Department of Prints and Drawings. She met Jacqueline when preparing the Victoria and Albert Museum's 1978 exhibition, *The Way We Live Now*. She had written to Jacqueline to request a loan of examples of her work and received, in return, an invitation to visit her studio. Margaret's visit resulted in Jacqueline lending several pieces of work to the exhibition and the museum subsequently purchased others from her. Margaret Timmers, like many before, and some after, was charmed by Jacqueline and became a good friend for the remainder of her life.[149]

Jacqueline would have been delighted by the inclusion of her work in both the exhibition and the permanent collection of the Victoria and Albert Museum, a serious academic recognition of her achievement. Yet further recognition was given in 1984 when the design historian and writer, Isabelle Anscombe, wrote of Jacqueline and her work in her survey of women designers.[150] Remarkably, a tape recording exists, over an hour in length, of an interview Isabelle had with Jacqueline when researching the book. By this time, 1981, she had moved to Ovington Square, Knightsbridge. Like Margaret Timmers, Isabelle also became a friend of Jacqueline's, who later gave Isabelle a beautiful, if somewhat whimsical, drawing as a gift when her daughter was born.

Towards the end of her life her legacy as a designer appears to have been very much on Jacqueline's mind. In her archive, now held in the Archive of Art and Design, the Victoria and Albert Museum, there are some rather pathetic lists written by her in a rackety hand on odd scraps of card or paper.[151] These seem to have been aides-memoires for her of the companies she had worked for, the exhibitions she had taken part in, the prizes she had won and the students she had taught. Most poignant is the mock-up of a proposed book of the highlights of her career, in which she dedicated a section to 'My Dolls', her constant companions. However, any fears she may have had of a complete eclipse of her work on her death would have been put to rest in 1984, when she was made an RDI, a Royal Designer For Industry, the ultimate accolade for any designer in Britain. In Jacqueline's case it was a long time coming. She was eighty-one when she at last achieved it, only two years before her death in 1986.

JACQUELINE GROAG PLATES

1 Left Design for a silk dress fabric, circa 1929, published in *Deutsche Kunst und Dekoration,* 1930.

2 Right Wallpaper design by Hilde Blumberger (Jacqueline Groag), circa 1929, and illustrated *Deutsche Kunst und Dekoration,* 1930.

3 Opposite Design for a printed silk by Hilde Blumberger (Jacqueline Groag), circa 1929, and illustrated in *Deutsche Kunst und Dekoration,* 1930.

4 Opposite Original artwork
for a design made by
Jacqueline whilst studying
with Hoffman in Vienna,
1929. A version was
subsequently exhibited at
*Historical and British
Wallpapers*, Suffolk Galleries,
1945. Courtesy V&A
images/Victoria & Albert
Museum, London

5 Left A group of the wooden dolls which gave Jacqueline such inspiration and were subsequently passed to Stefan Buzas' daughter Kate. Courtesy of Kate Irvine

6 Opposite Jacqueline used her dolls for numerous designs and often drew on them for inspiration. This charcoal drawing of a wooden doll was a preparatory sketch for her design *Toys,* now in the Victoria & Albert Museum, Prints and Drawings Department. Collection H. Kirk Brown III and Jill A. Wiltse

7 Previous page and Opposite
Undated design by Jacqueline, inscribed *Toys* and numbered
41. Courtesy V&A Images/Victoria & Albert Museum, London

8 Above In this painting, from
about 1966, Jacqueline's usual
grid structure is less obvious
but the artwork and colour
combination is closely related
to the *Paper Dolls* fabric for
John Lewis designed in 1967.
Collection H. Kirk Brown III
and Jill A. Wiltse

9 Opposite Design for
a textile, circa 1954.
This design is related to
Groag's furnishing fabric for
Jonelle, produced in 1967.
It illustrates her deceptively
naïve, almost childlike
drawing inspired by her
teacher Prof Franz Cizek.
Collection H. Kirk Brown III
and Jill A. Wiltse

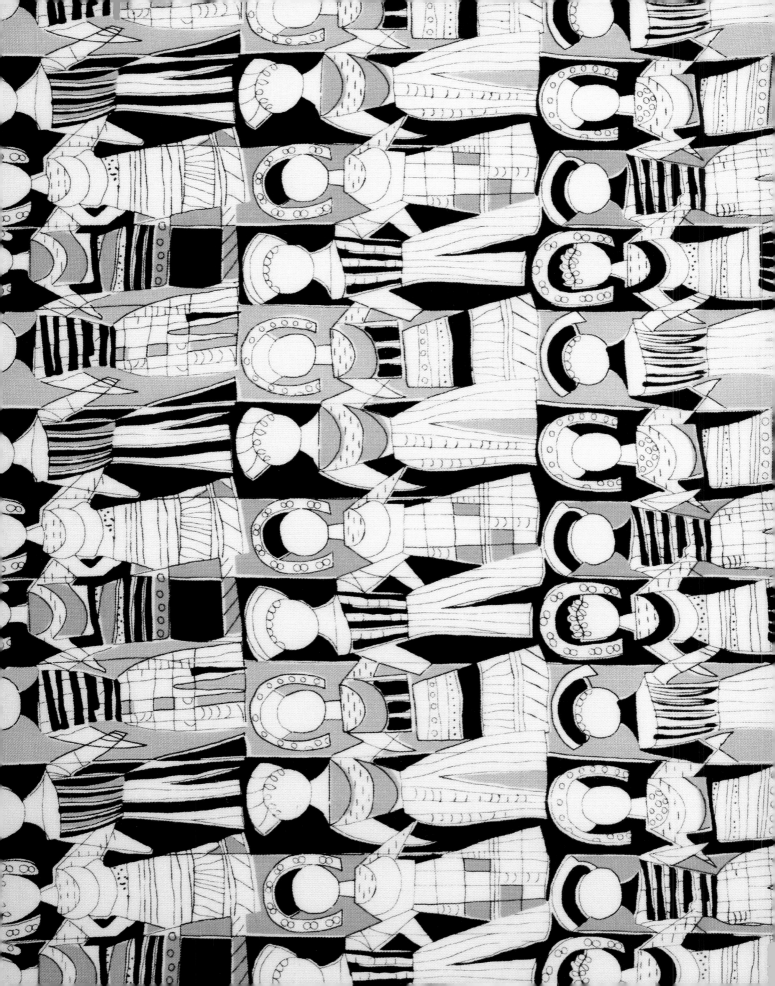

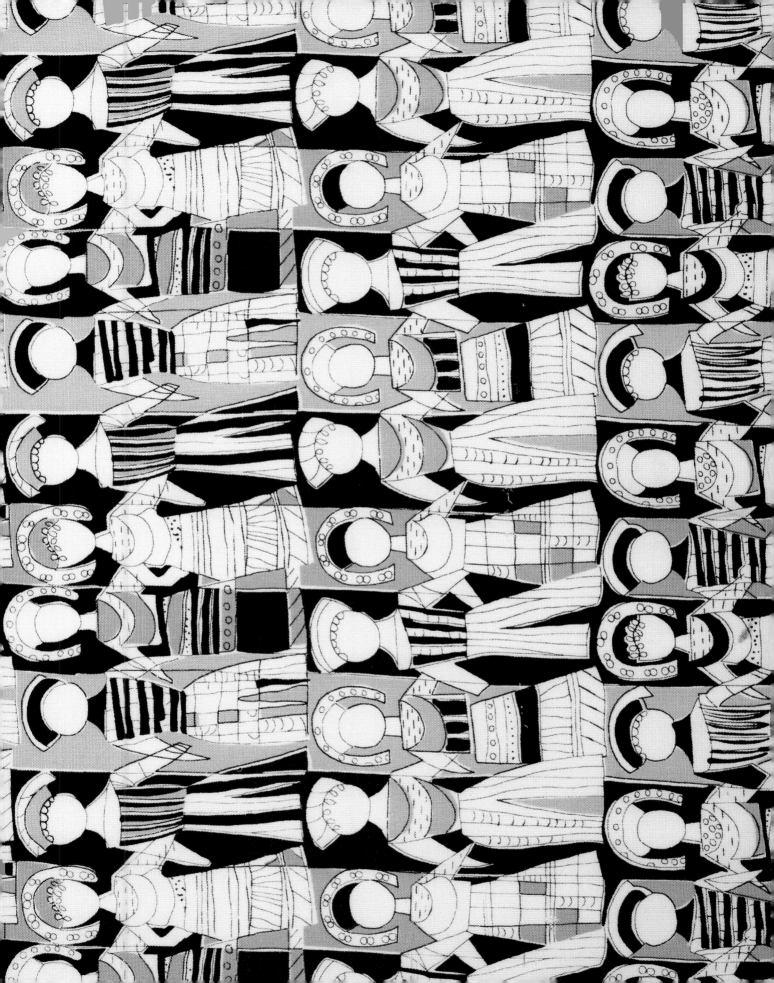

11 Left Artwork for *Beauty Contest,*
a textile design by Jacqueline for
the Rayon Design Centre, circa
1948 and illustrated in *Designers
in Britain,* 1949. Courtesy V&A
Images/Victoria & Albert Museum,
London

12 Right A textile design illustrated
in *The Ambassador,* 1946.

13 Top left *Slavonika,* a textile design illustrated in Professor Charles Reilly's article in *Art & Industry,* 1942, entitled 'Design for textiles – the work of Jacqueline Groag'. *Slavonika,* the Dvorak ballet, was premiered the previous year and was travelling the USA in 1942.

14 Bottom left *Rendez-vous,* a two-colour design for a dress fabric published in *Art & Industry,* 1942.

15 Opposite A textile design typical of Jacqueline's work of the early 1940s. Collection H. Kirk Brown III and Jill A. Wiltse

16 Opposite Textile design
dating from 1943-4 and
illustrated in *International
Textiles,* the forerunner
to *The Ambassador,* 1945.
The article, entitled 'Prehistoric
Topics,' featured a number
of designs by Jacqueline.

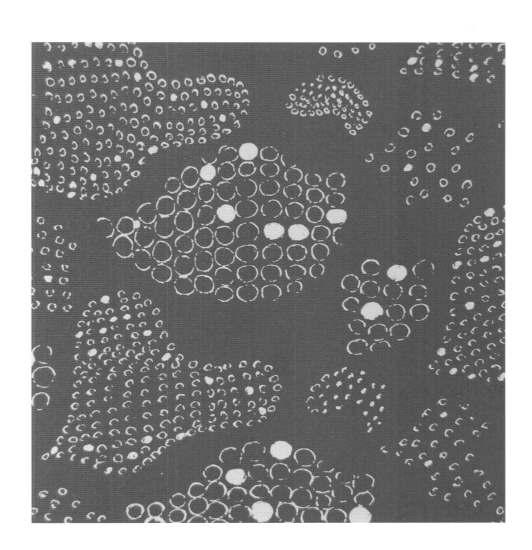

17 Opposite A printed cotton dress fabric, circa 1940.

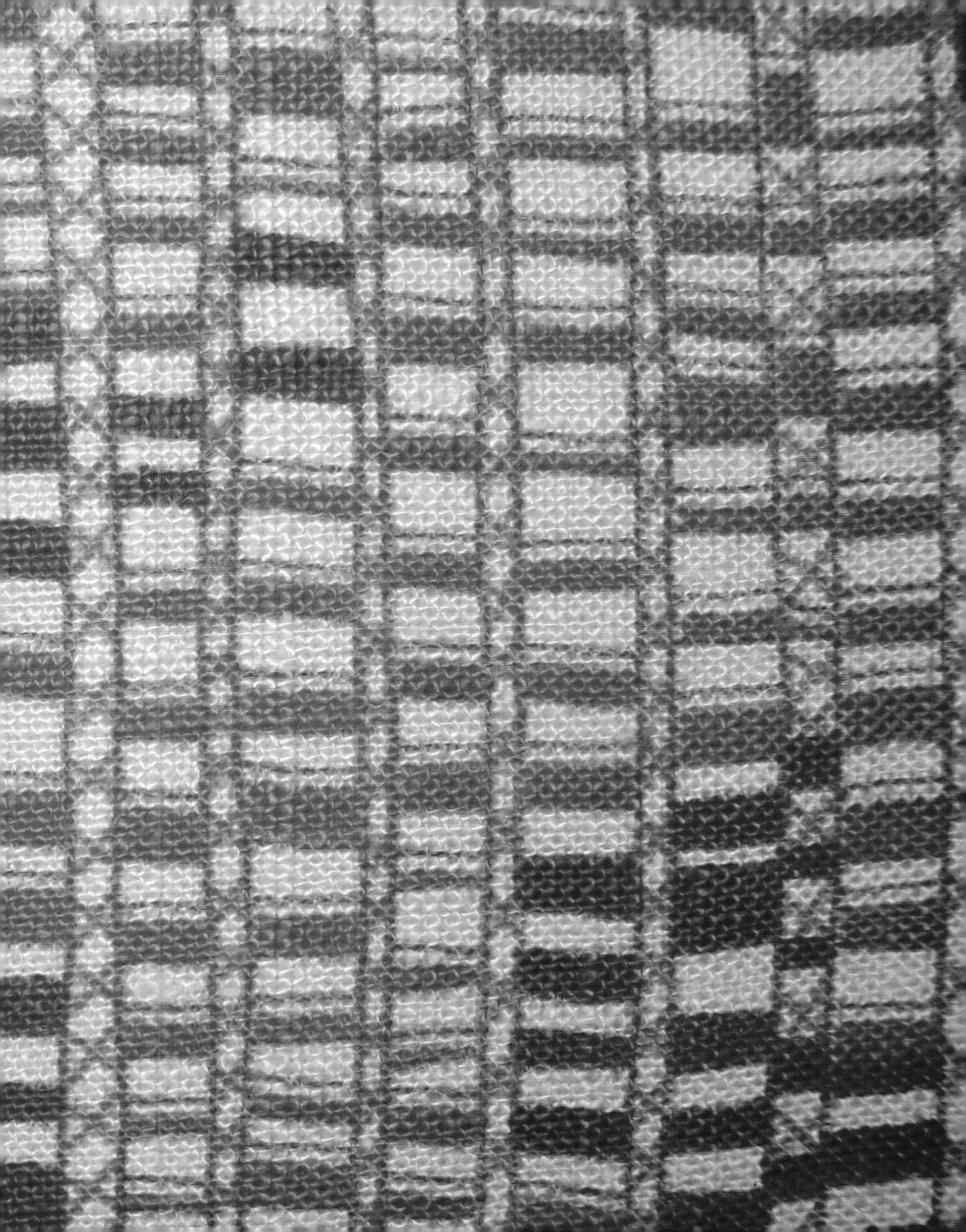

18 Top left Printed rayon satin dress fabric designed for F.W. Grafton & Co. Ltd, c.1946. The design of this textile is based on the Island of Arbe, on the Dalmatian coast. This Italian/Croatian island was an inspiration for Jacqueline for numerous textiles and wallpapers from the late 1920s onwards.

19 Bottom left A design illustrated in *The Ambassador,* 1946. The article comments: 'textile designs by Jacqueline Groag shows her tendency to take inspiration from real life, rather than slavishly copying reality'.

20 Opposite A printed cotton fabric for Grafton with a *Calpreta* finish. *Carefree Calpreta,* marketed through the Calico Printers Association, promised to remain crumple free, non-shrink and with a permanent sheen, glaze or lustre that would make the post-war housewife's life easier and more fun. *Calpreta* was one of a number of textile finishes developed by chemical companies to make domestic life for women less arduous as lives became more busy and domestic staff less common.

21 Previous page Printed nylon dress fabric, produced by F.W. Grafton, 1946.

22 Below Dress fabric designed for Stevenson & Son's Moygashel range and illustrated in *The Ambassador,* 1946.

23 Opposite Roller-printed rayon textile produced by Stevenson & Son for their Moygashel range, circa 1946.

24 Left Design for a dress
fabric, subsequently
produced by Stevenson
& Son, for their Moygashel
range and illustrated in
The Ambassador, 1946.

25 Opposite A textile design,
circa 1943. Private Collection

26 Previous spread one A printed rayon dress fabric probably by Grafton designed by Jacqueline circa 1946. Jacqueline designed a range of dress fabrics for Grafton including a tulip design subsequently made up by the couturier Edward Molyneux for HRH Princess Elizabeth. Private Collection

27 Previous spread two Printed 'anti-shrink' crepe dress fabric produced by F.W. Grafton, circa 1946. Private Collection.

28 Previous spread three Printed floral dress fabric for F.W. Grafton, 1940s. Private Collection

29 Opposite Floral design, 1950s. An outstanding example of Jacqueline's use of collage and mixed media. Collection H. Kirk Brown III and Jill A. Wiltse

Jacqueline

30 Previous page Roller-printed rayon furnishing fabric, adapted from Jacqueline's textile for the Festival Information Centre and produced by David Whitehead for the mass market, 1952.

31 Opposite Detail of the three-dimensional screen designed by Jacqueline for the *Living World* section of the *Dome of Discovery* at the Festival of Britain, 1951.

32 Opposite One of
Jacqueline's earliest designs
for David Whitehead, printed
on satinised cotton, circa
1952. This relatively expensive
fabric was one of the –
company's more exclusive
furnishing textiles.
Collection H. Kirk Brown III
and Jill A. Wiltse.

33 Over page Textile design with an abstract sculptural
theme, printed on rayon by David Whitehead, circa 1953.
Collection H. Kirk Brown III and Jill A. Wiltse

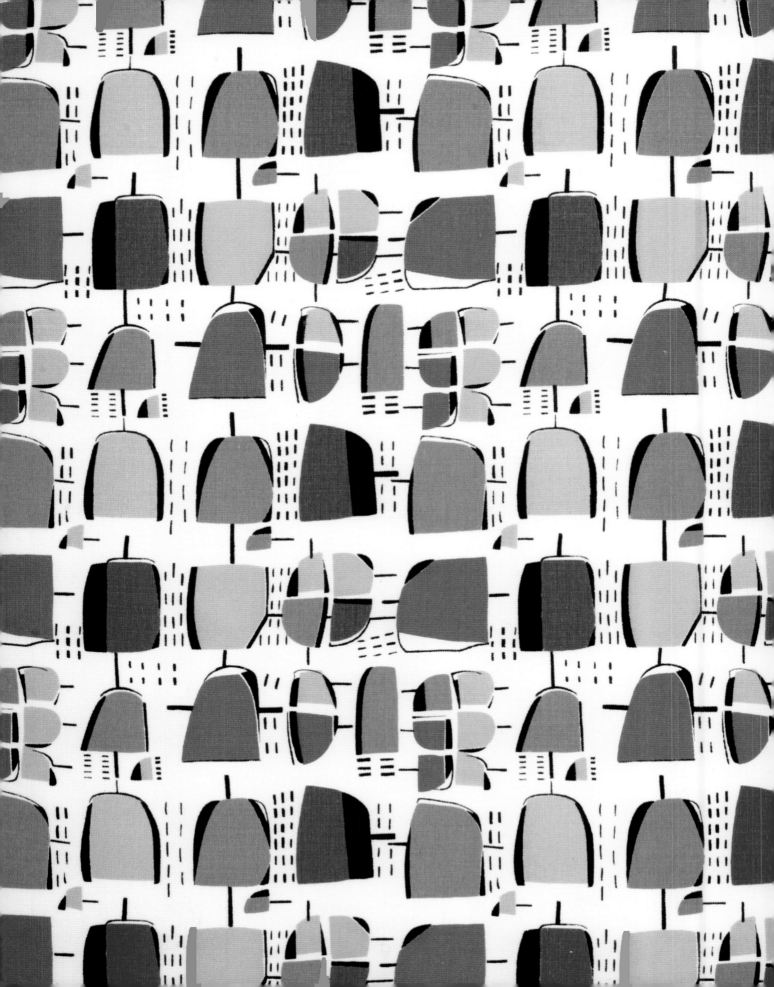

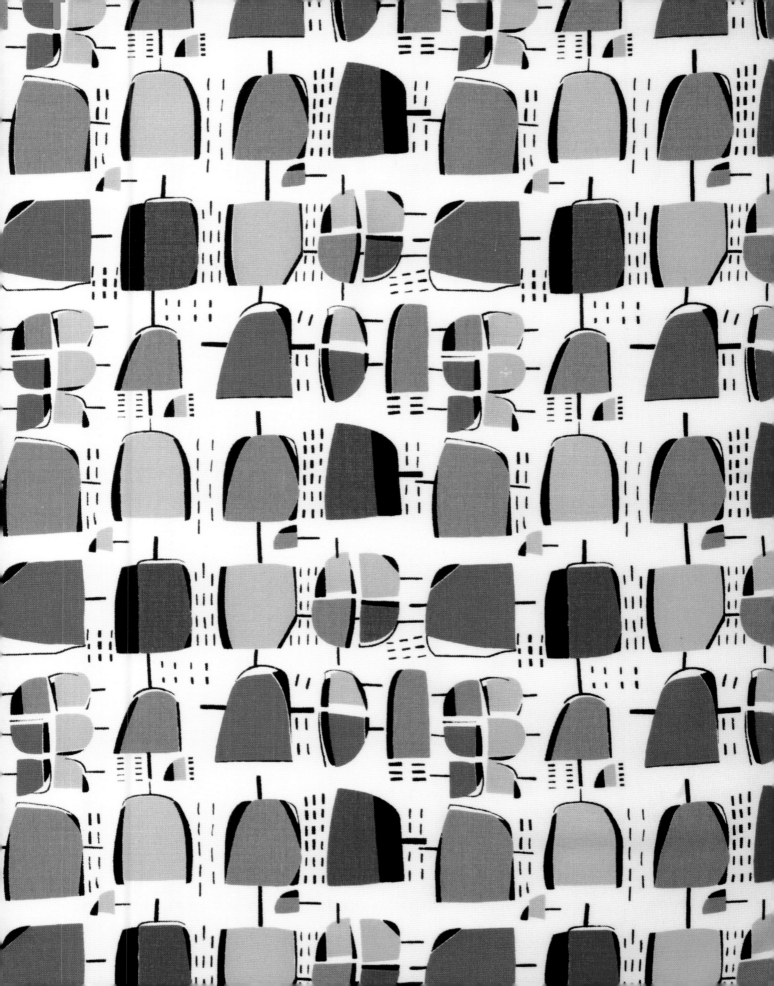

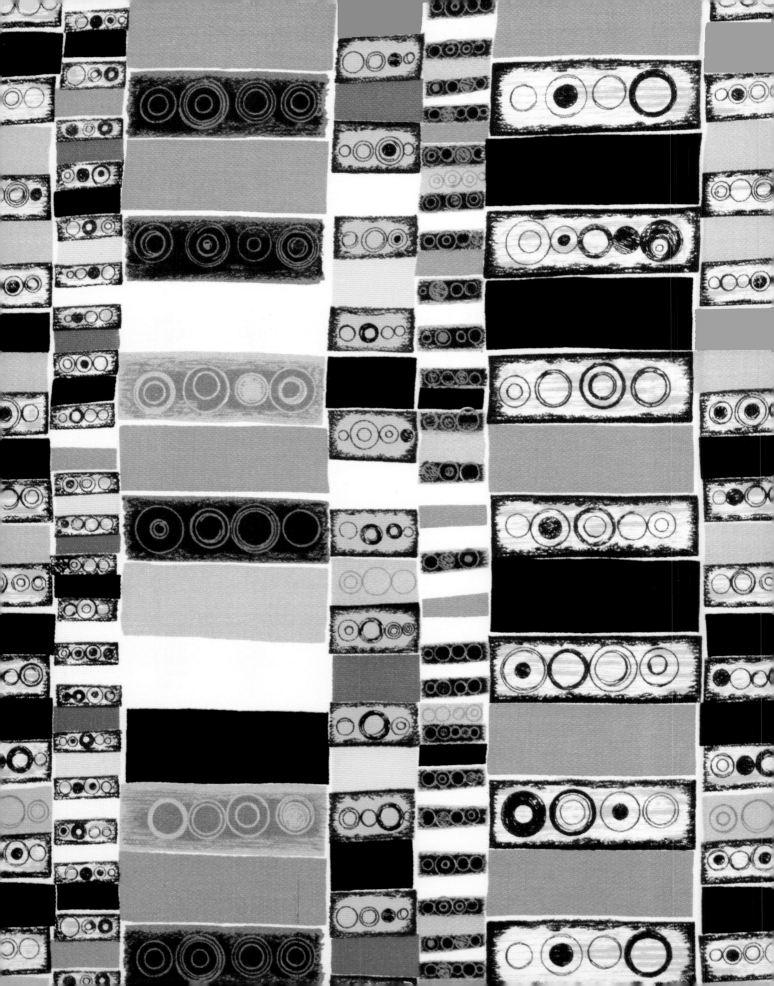

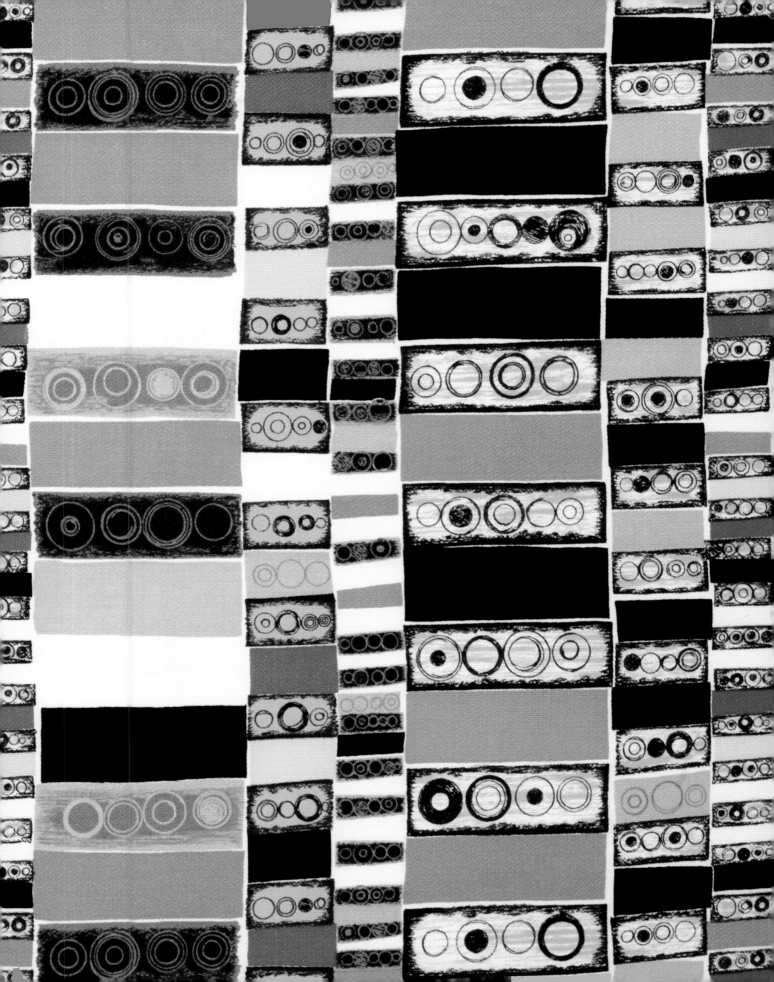

34 Previous page Roller-printed spun rayon furnishing fabric for David Whitehead, circa 1953. This is one of Jacqueline's most popular designs, which even found its way on to ticking for mattresses for Myers beds. Collection H. Kirk Brown III and Jill A. Wiltse

35 Opposite Drawing for a grid pattern design, probably for a textile. Collection H. Kirk Brown III and Jill A. Wiltse

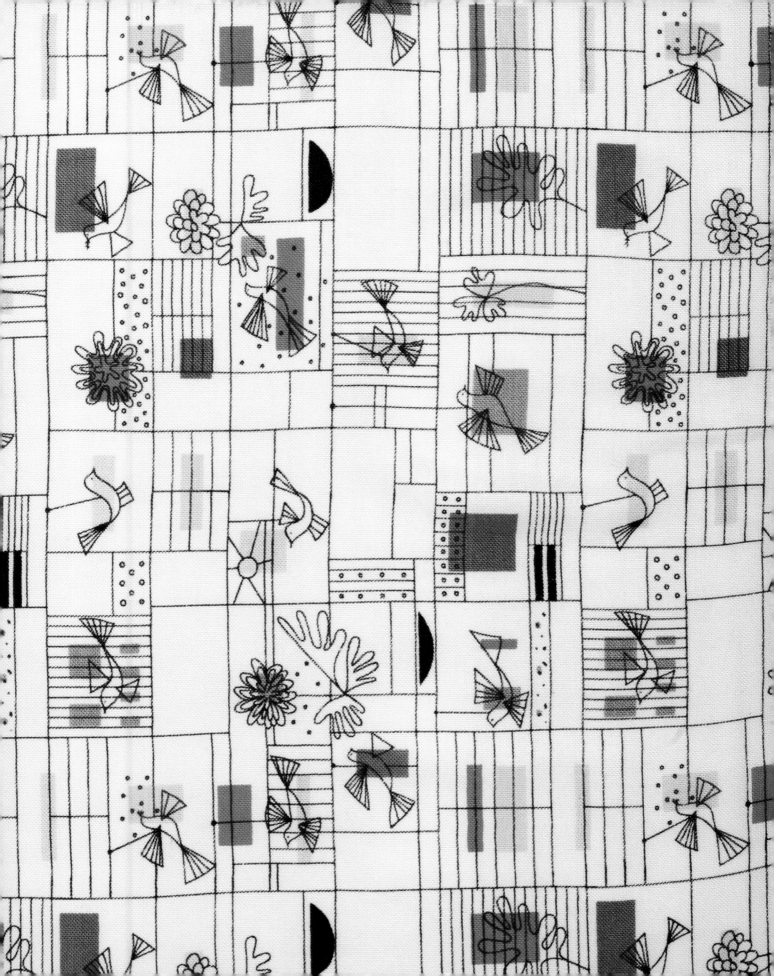

36 Previous spread one Floral and bird design roller-printed on their distinctive spun rayon fabric by Haworth Fabrics, 1953. Collection H. Kirk Brown III and Jill A. Wiltse

37 Previous spread two Floral design roller-printed spun rayon fabric by Haworth Fabrics, 1953. Collection H. Kirk Brown III and Jill A. Wiltse

38 Below Flowers were a favourite theme of Jacqueline's and tulips particularly so. This drawing using a grid structure shows how Jacqueline built up her repeat patterns. Collection H. Kirk Brown III and Jill A. Wiltse

39 Previous page Roller-printed rayon furnishing fabric produced by David Whitehead, circa 1952 and attributed to Jacqueline. Collection H. Kirk Brown III and Jill A. Wiltse

40 Opposite Pen and ink drawing for a textile design for David Whitehead, inscribed 'one ground with colour'. A second version of this design is in the Victoria and Albert Museum's collection. The resulting textile is illustrated in the *Studio Yearbook of Decorative Art,* 1954-5. Collection H. Kirk Brown III and Jill A. Wiltse

one ~~plate~~ ground with colour

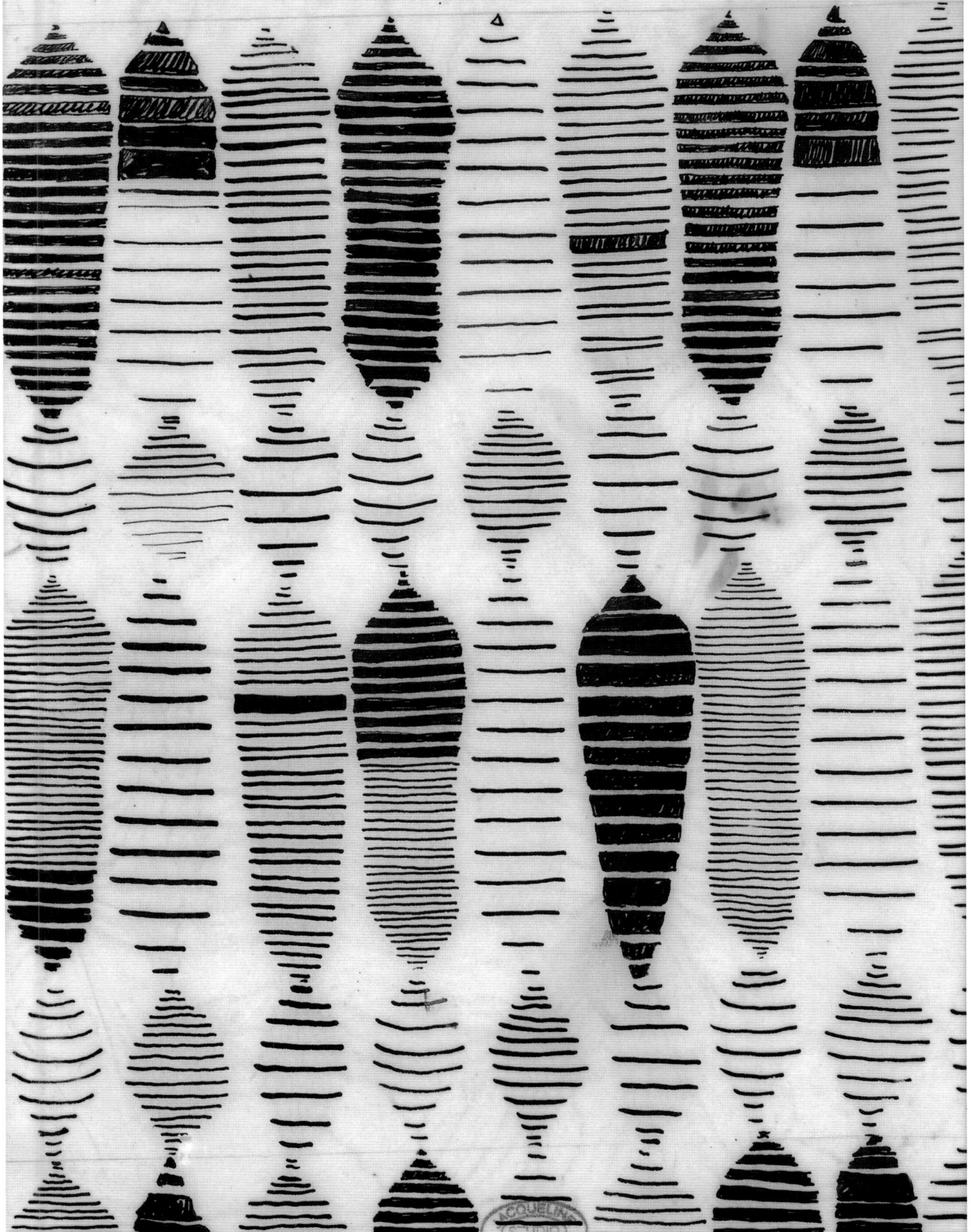

41 Opposite Printed cotton dress fabric, circa 1956, produced for the American market. Collection H. Kirk Brown III and Jill A. Wiltse

42, 43 *Duet,* a printed cotton
dress fabric by Associated
American Artists, 1954.
Private Collection

44 Opposite *Enchanted Garden,* a printed cotton dress fabric, in three colourways by Associated American Artists, 1954. Private Collection

45 Opposite *Toy Parade,*
a printed cotton by
Associated American Artists,
circa 1955, for their
'Signature' range of dress
fabrics. Collection H. Kirk
Brown III and Jill A. Wiltse

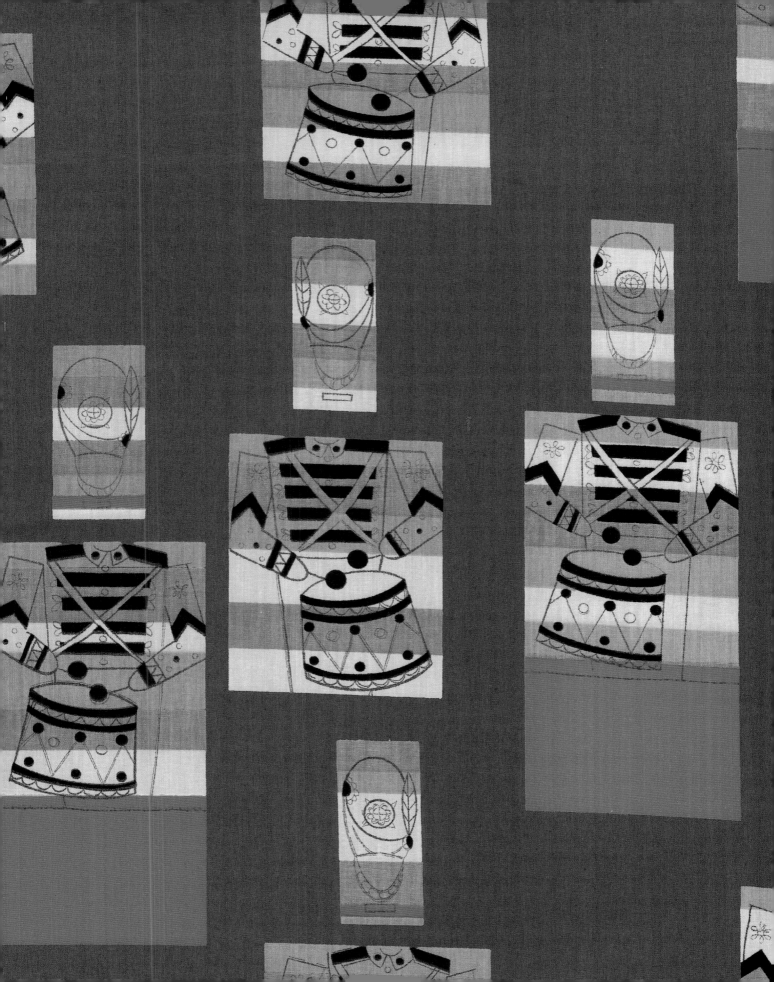

46 Opposite *Puppet Ballet* was produced for the US market by Associated American Artists in 1953 as a printed cotton dress fabric in their 'Signature' range. Like *Kiddies Town* it illustrates Jacqueline's deceivingly naïve drawing combined with a sophisticated pattern structure. Collection H. Kirk Brown III and Jill A. Wiltse

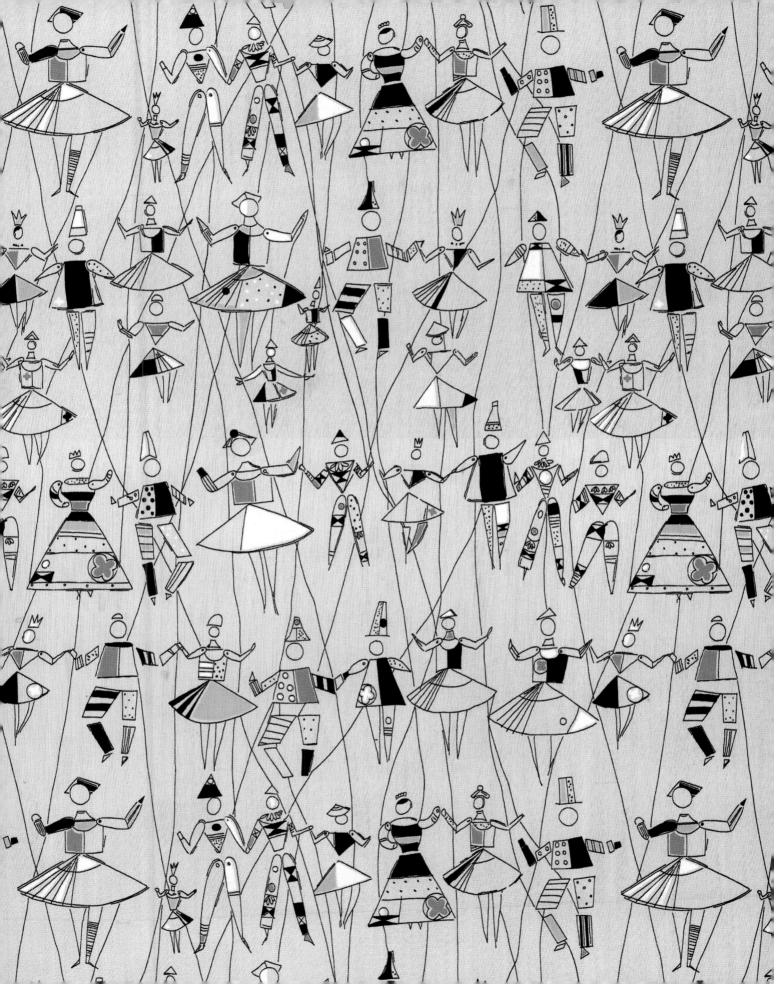

47 Top left Design for printed cotton fabric for Associated American Artists, 1957.

48 Bottom Left Printed cotton textile designed by Jacqueline for Associated American Artists, 1950s.

49 Opposite *Calico Tulips,* a printed dress fabric for Associated American Artists, 1953. Kate Irvine recalls that vases of white tulips were frequently placed around Jacqueline's home. Courtesy of Francesca Galloway Ltd

50 Previous page A collage design for Delsey Fabrics, New York, 1958 in two colourways. Collection H. Kirk Brown III and Jill A. Wiltse

51 Opposite *Cleo,* a textile design, annotated on the reverse 'Sold/U.S'. Courtesy of the Victoria and Albert Museum

52 Above *Trellis,* a printed cotton for Warner & Sons, circa 1955. Jacqueline designed at least three textiles for Warner & Sons.

53 Opposite *Purbeck,* a printed textile design for Warner & Sons published in *Designers in Britain,* 1956. The design was created using a hand-cut lino block which, alongside a number of others, remains in the Archive of Art & Design, Victoria and Albert Museum, London

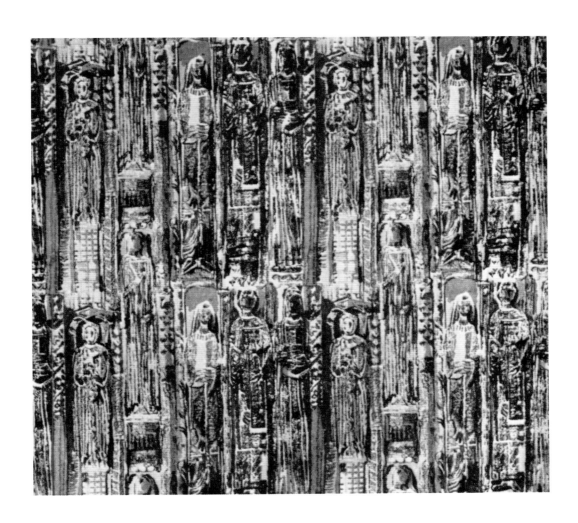

54 Opposite *Belmoral,*
a wallpaper for Arthur
Sanderson & Son, circa 1955.

55 Opposite *Grasses,* a design for BOAC for multiple use in aircraft interiors. It was inspired by a print in an 1820 encyclopaedia and would have been commissioned from Jacqueline by Gaby Schreiber, the interior designer responsible for BOAC aircraft interiors. The design was used on decorative wall panels made from Synthede and a pvc coated fabric, Leonide, both produced by Jas. Williamson & Son.

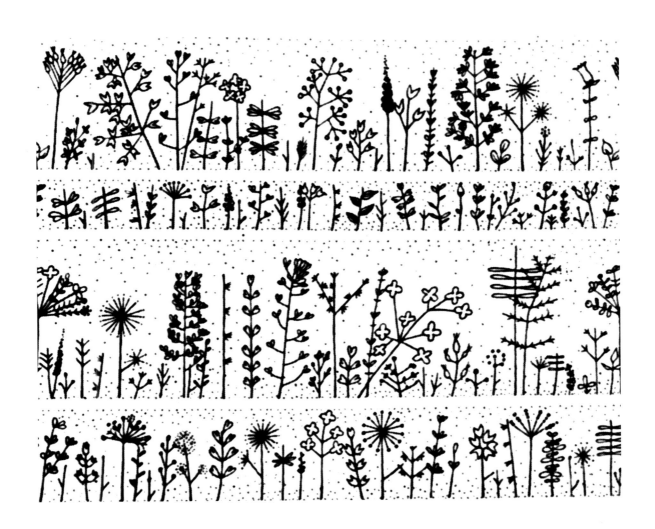

56 Opposite A multiple
purpose Christmas card,
hanging decoration or crib
figure. Sgraffito decorated
gold card, early 1960s.
Jacqueline's notes in
the Archive of Art and
Design, London, mention
a 'cut-out golden angel'
she designed for Oxfam/
Unicef. Collection H. Kirk
Brown III and Jill A. Wiltse

57 Opposite Abstract design,
probably for a greetings card,
1960s. Collection H. Kirk
Brown III and Jill A. Wiltse.

58 Opposite Artwork for
a Valentine's Day card,
probably for Hallmark Cards,
1960s. Collection H. Kirk Brown
III and Jill A. Wiltse

59 Over page Artwork, probably for gift-wrapping paper,
possibly for Coloroll, 1960s. Collection H. Kirk Brown III and
Jill A. Wiltse

Jacqueline

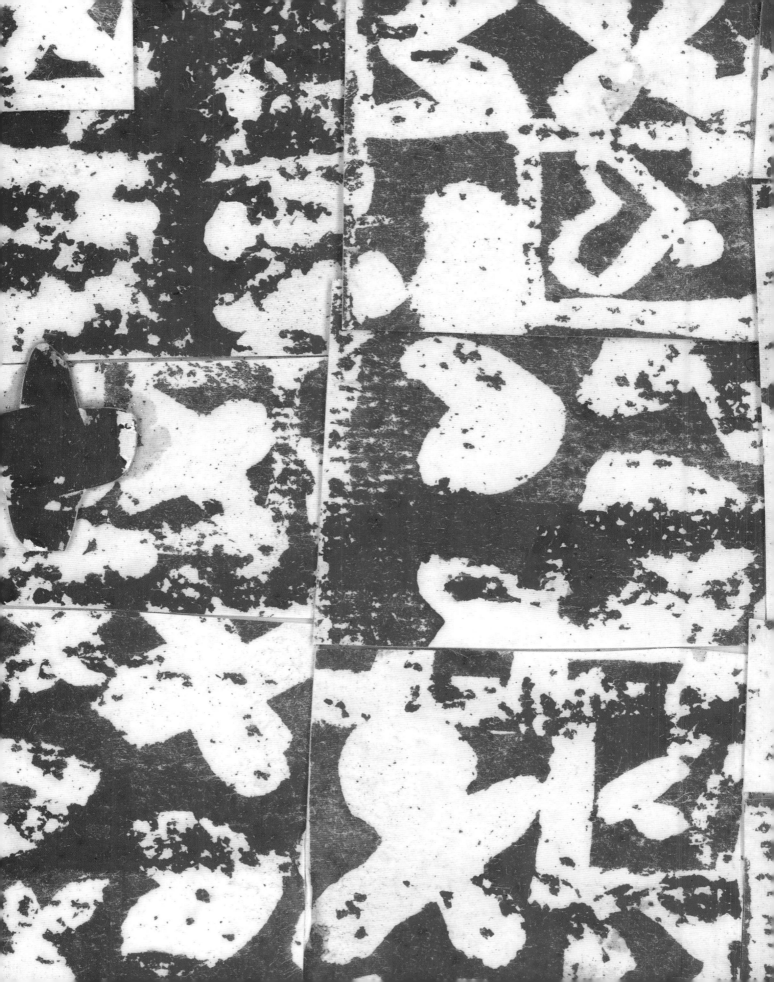

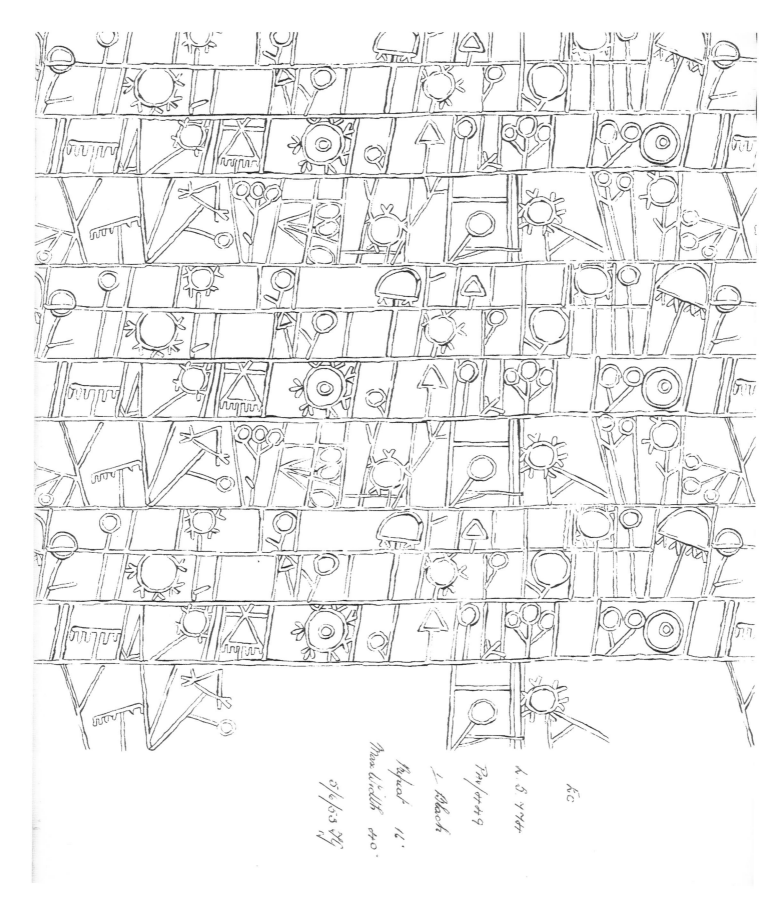

60 Previous page, left Paper strike-off for printed Ardil, a man-made fabric, produced by ICI and printed at either Liberty's Merton Abbey or Langley Printworks in about 1954. Courtesy of the Liberty Archive

61 Previous page, right *Alphabeth*, a preliminary design for Ardil, 1950s. Collection H. Kirk Brown III and Jill A. Wiltse

62 Opposite Small-scale naïve design for a man-made fabric, possibly for ICI's *Ardil* range of nursery textiles, 1954. Collection H. Kirk Brown III and Jill A. Wiltse

63 Over page *Books*. A paper strike-off for a textile design for Liberty of London, 1954. *Books* was marketed under the *Young Liberty* range, alongside designs by Robert Stewart and Lucienne Day. Courtesy Liberty Archive

64 Above Advertising material
for Warerite, showing
Jacqueline's *Exotica* and
Mezzola laminate designs.

65 Above *Manhattan,*
a plastic laminate produced
by Warerite in 1959. One of
Jacqueline's best selling
laminate patterns of the
1950s and 1960s, it was used
by many British furniture
manufacturers for washable
decorative surfaces on tables
and cabinets.

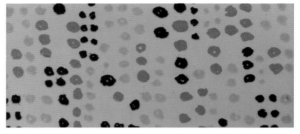

66 *Speculo,* a plastic laminate
produced by Warerite in 1959

67 *Mezzola,* a plastic laminate
produced by Warerite in 1959

68 *Murano,* a plastic laminate
produced by Warerite in 1959

69 *Domino,* a plastic laminate
produced by Warerite in 1959

70 Opposite Collage design
for a laminate, circa 1960

71 Opposite Cover for *Design,*
the Council of Industrial
Design's magazine, November
1959, showing Jacqueline's
Metropolis laminate for
Warerite. In this issue of
the monthly magazine is
a feature on the design
of British Rail trains for the
Glasgow Suburban Railways.
The interior detailing and
finishes were overseen by
Misha Black of the Design
Research Unit who
commissioned Jacqueline
to design patterned
laminates for wall panels
produced by Formica Ltd.

The Council of Industrial Design

November 1959   No 131   Price 3s

Design

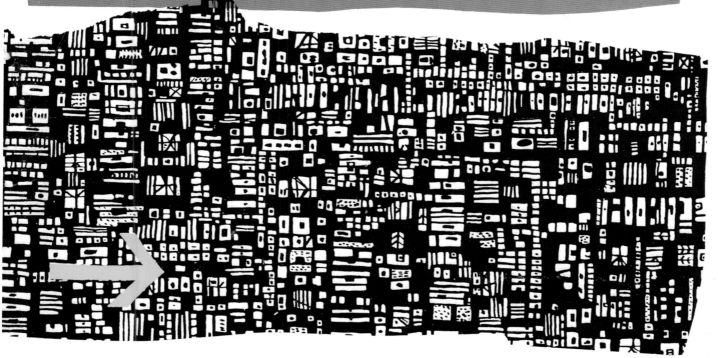

THOMPSON

72 Opposite A collage design
for plastic laminate created
using printed photographic
images, circa 1959.
Collection H. Kirk Brown III
and Jill A. Wiltse

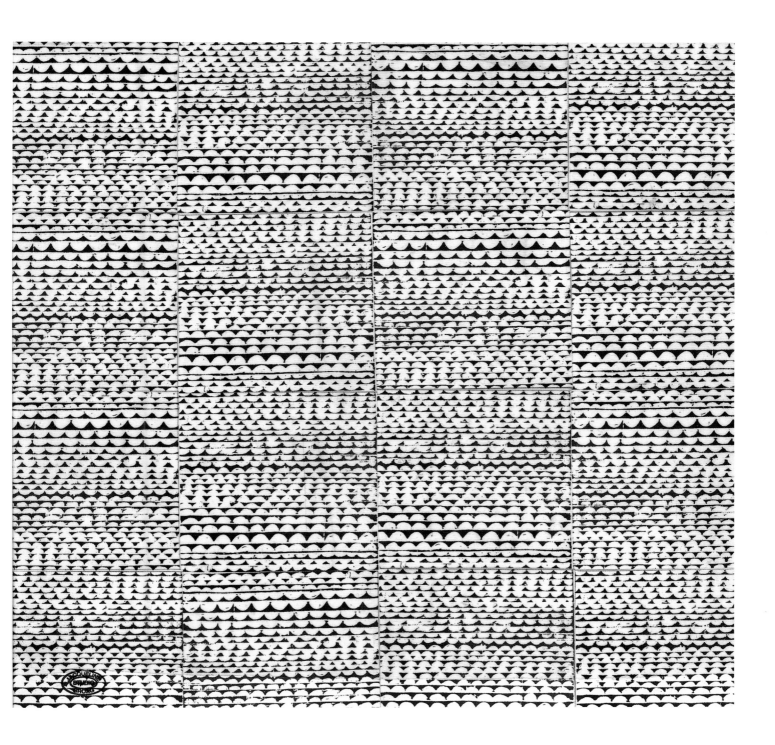

73 Opposite Laminate design
for Harrison & Sons, 1960s.

74 Opposite Advertising material
for Bond Worth's fabrics and
carpets illustrating five of
Jacqueline's carpets for the
firm's *Augustine* range, 1958.

SPECTRUM fabrics

Canterbury

York

Winchester

Stirling

partners in harmony

Tessella

Parterre

Manhattan

Numidia

Lapidia

bond worth CARPETS

All Bond Worth carpets are mothproofed · These Spectrum Fabrics are 'Sanforized' shrunk

See the new designs now on display at many furnishing stores · Cut-length service is offered for both products

THOMAS BOND WORTH & SONS LTD STOURPORT-ON-SEVERN · WORCS · SPECTRUM FABRICS LTD · WALTER STREET · BLACKBURN · LANCS

TGA B513

75 Opposite *Oysterbay,*
an Axminster carpet designed
by Jacqueline for Andrew Gaskell,
Lancashire, 1966, and illustrated
in the firm's promotional
material. In *Design,* 1968,
the manufacturer stated that
Jacqueline had been given
complete artistic freedom
to achieve the end effect.

76 Right *Magenta,* an Axminster
carpet for Andrew Gaskell,
Lancashire, 1966, from the
firm's promotional material.

77 **Previous page** Printed woollen dress fabric, circa 1967, probably for John Lewis. Collection H. Kirk Brown III and Jill A. Wiltse

78 **Above** Paper dress with a printed pattern designed by Jacqueline Groag circa 1967. **Opposite** Original magazine advertisement, circa 1967.

79 **Over page** Satinised cotton furnishing fabric, by Cavendish Textiles, a division of John Lewis, 1950s. Jacqueline's involvement with John Lewis dates back to the 1940s: in 1946 the store exhibited three designs by her at the *Britain Can Make It* exhibition at the Victoria and Albert Museum. This design relates to her work for Kardomah Cafés, circa 1949, which was commissioned by Misha Black and the DRU. Collection H. Kirk Brown III and Jill A. Wiltse

what's so
different
about this
dress?

**Surprise!
it's paper**
and comes with
a party
to match!

The invitation matches the party centerpiece. The centerpiece
matches the plates, cups, coasters, napkins, place cards, table-
cloths and place mats. The table settings match the snack
bowls. The snack bowls match the gift wrap on the party gift.
The gift wrap matches the bridge tallies, table covers and
matchbooks. And the whole Flower Fantasy party matches
your swinging new paper party dress.

After the party and the compliments you can toss it all away
and relax! It's another colorful new party idea from Hallmark
stylists. You'll find everything, including the dress, now at
fine stores that feature Hallmark cards.

Hallmark
Plans-a-Party
**Fun for everyone—
including
the hostess**

83 Opposite Abstract design
incorporating floral motifs
on a printed cotton dress
fabric, probably for
John Lewis, 1970s.
Private Collection

84 Opposite *Tinkerbell,*
a printed cotton furnishing
fabric for John Lewis,
printed 1968. Courtesy of
the John Lewis Partnership
Archive Collection

87 Above *Dandini,* artwork for
a cotton furnishing fabric for
John Lewis, printed in 1971.
Courtesy of the John Lewis
Partnership Archive Collection

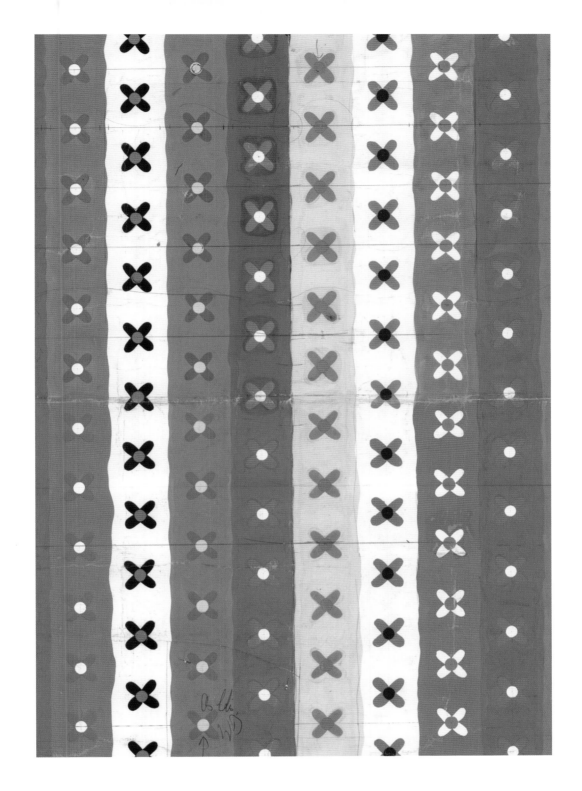

88 Above *Multistripe,* artwork
for a furnishing fabric for
John Lewis, first printed in the
1950s and re-issued in 1973.
Courtesy of the John Lewis
Partnership Archive Collection

89 Opposite *Aquarius,*
a cotton furnishing fabric for
John Lewis, printed in 1969.
Courtesy of the John Lewis
Partnership Archive Collection

90 Previous page *Telstar,* a cotton furnishing fabric for John Lewis, printed in 1970. Courtesy of the John Lewis Partnership Archive Collection

91 Opposite Collage design for a montage in the starboard lounge of *St. Edmund*, the British Rail Sealink Ferry between Harwich and The Hook of Holland, circa 1975. Courtesy V&A Images/Victoria and Albert Museum, London

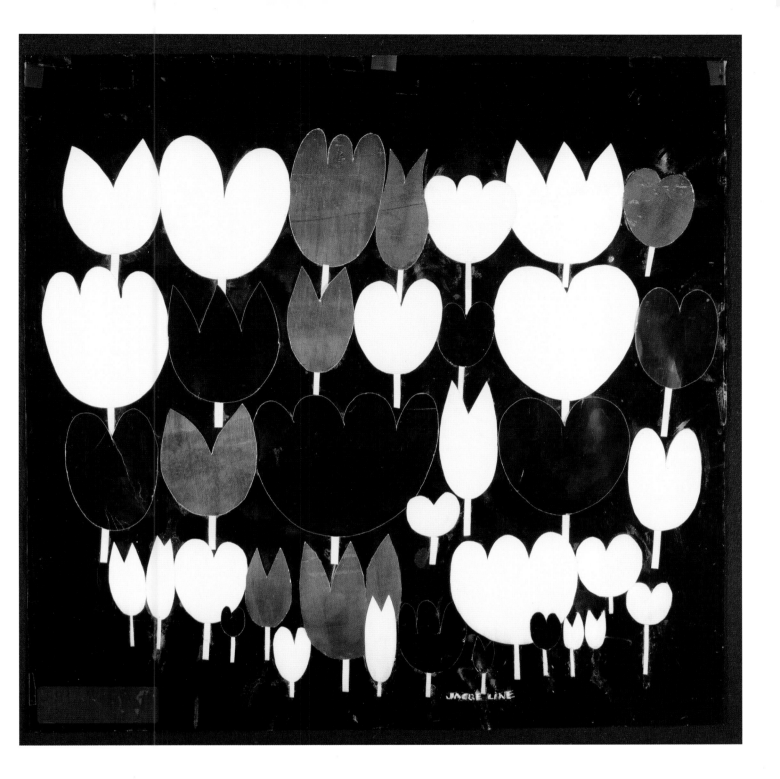

APPENDICES

Textiles for UK Companies

F.W. Grafton & Co Ltd
dress and furnishing fabrics, 1940s and 1950s.
Grafton were part of the Calico Printers
Association (CPA) and designs produced by
the company were often referred
to by Groag as 'printed by the CPA'.

Messrs Hill Brown Ltd
furnishing fabrics, 1940s and 1950s

John Lewis Ltd
dress and furnishing fabrics, 1940s to 1970s
produced under the names Cavendish
Textiles or Jonelle

John Heathcoat & Co
dress fabrics, 1940s

Stevenson & Son Ltd (Moygashel)
dress fabrics, 1940s

Gerald Holtom
furnishing fabrics, 1940s

David Whitehead Ltd
furnishing fabrics, 1950s

A. Warner & Son Ltd
furnishing fabrics, 1950s

Edinburgh Weavers Ltd
furnishing fabrics, 1950s

Haworth Fabrics Ltd
furnishing fabrics, 1950s

Horrockses Fashions Ltd
dress fabrics, 1950s

Liberty of London
dress and furnishing fabrics,
1950s and early 1960s

ICI Ltd (Imperial Chemical Industries Ltd)
furnishing fabrics, some printed
through Liberty of London

Charnos
dress fabric, 1960s

Textiles for European Companies

Chanel
Paris, handprinted dress silks, 1930s

Lanvin
Paris, handprinted dress silks, 1930s

Paul Poiret
Paris, handprinted dress silks, 1930s

Schiaparelli
Paris, handprinted dress silks, 1930s

Worth
Paris, handprinted dress silks, 1930s

Rodier
France furnishing fabrics, 1930s

Göppinger Kaliko und Kunstlerderwerke GmbH
Germany furnishing fabrics, 1950s

Textiles for USA Companies

Associated American Artists
dress fabrics for the 'Signature' range, 1950s,
manufactured by M. Lowenstein & Co

Isabel Scott Fabrics Corp
New York dress fabrics, 1950s

Delsey Fabrics
New York, 1950s

Reeves Brothers Inc
New York, 1950s

Heyter
New York, 1950s

Wallpapers for UK Companies

John Line Ltd
1950s

A. Sanderson & Son Ltd
1950s

Wallpaper Manufacturers Ltd (WPM)
1950s

Coloroll
wallpaper and packaging,
1960s and 1970s

Wallpapers for European Companies

Rasch
Germany 1950s

Sandudd Vantaa
Finland 1970s

Floor Coverings for UK Companies

Bond Worth Ltd
carpets, 1950s

Andrew Gaskell Ltd
carpets, 1960s

Scott Linoleum Ltd

Graphic Design for UK Companies

Ambassador Publications
cover designs,
1940s and 1950s

James Valentine & Sons Ltd, Dundee
greetings cards, 1950s and 1960s

Oxfam/Unicef
greetings cards, 1960s

Thomas De La Rue Ltd
playing cards, 1960s

Liberty of London
matchbooks etc., 1950s and 1960s

Graphic Design for USA Companies

Hallmark Cards Inc
New York (also for Hallmark, Paris)
greetings cards, 1950s and 1960s

American Greetings
Ohio, greetings cards and wrapping papers,
1950s and 1960s

Interiors **Magazine**
cover design, 1950s

Plastic Laminates for UK Companies

Formica Ltd (De La Rue)
1950s

Warerite (Bakelite Group)
1950s and 1960s

Harrison & Sons Ltd
1960s

Plastic Laminates for European Companies

Perstorp
Sweden, 1950s and 1960s

Industrial Design and Interior Design Projects

British Rail and Sealink
patterned plastic laminates for panelling, table
tops etc., 1950s; decorated metal lampshades
decorative hand-coloured wall panels for the
'Silver Train', 1960; wall coverings for Sealink
ferries, 1970s; all in association with the Design
Research Unit (DRU)

London Transport
textiles in association with the DRU,
1960s and 1970s

A.H. Holt Shipping Co Ltd
designs for interiors for cargo boats and ocean
steam ships in association with the architect
Neville Ward, 1950s

British Holland & Channel Line

BOAC (British Overseas Airways Corporation)
laminates and plastic coated fabrics for panelling,
fabrics for seating etc., 1950s and 1960s in
association with Gaby Schreiber Associates

BEA (British Empire Airlines)
interiors for coaches, 1950s and 1960s

Kardomah Cafés Ltd
textiles and graphic design,
1940s to 1950 in association with the DRU

Dunlop Ltd
textiles, 1950s in association
with the DRU

Other Companies

Lomond Ltd

Johnson, Matthey & Co Ltd
silk screen designs for ceramics, 1950s

Standard Telephone & Cable
London

Munro

Exhibitions and Awards

Salzburg Festival, 1929
first prize for a poster design

Wiener Werkstätte, 1929
first prize for textile design

Exposition Colonial, Paris, 1931
gold medal awarded for lace designs

The Milan Triennale, Italy, 1933
gold medal awarded for nine textile designs

The World Fair, Paris, 1937
gold medal awarded for printed textiles

**The Centre for Colour, Design and Style,
Cotton Board, Manchester, 1941**
textiles

**Historical & British Wallpapers,
The Suffolk Galleries, London, 1945**
wallpaper designs

***Britain Can Make It*, The Victoria and
Albert Museum, London 1946**
textiles

Member of the Society of Industrial Artists, 1947
subsequently made a Fellow of the Society

**The Festival of Britain, the South Bank,
London, 1951**
textiles and wallpapers, three-dimensional
sculptural screen for the *Living World* section
of the *Dome of Discovery*

***Painting Into Textiles*, The Institute of
Contemporary Art, London 1953**
textile designs

Starpacks competition, 1963
highest award for playing cards and
packaging for De La Rue

***The Way We Live Now*, Victoria and
Albert Museum, London, 1978**
textiles and textile design

Appointed a Royal Designer for Industry in 1984

Bibliography

Books

Anscombe, Isabelle, *A Woman's Touch: Women in Design from 1860 to the Present Day,* Virago Press Ltd, London, 1984.

Brandstatter, Christian, *Wonderful Wiener Werkstätte: Design in Vienna 1903-1932,* Thames and Hudson Ltd, London, 2003.

Byars, Mel, *The Design Encyclopedia,* Laurence King Publishing, London, 1994.

Carrington, Noel, *Design And Decoration in the Home,* B.T. Batsford Ltd, London, 1952.

Chatwin, Bruce, *Utz,* Jonathan Cape Ltd, London, 1988.

Collins, Judith, *The Omega Workshops,* Martin Secker and Warburg Ltd, London, 1983.

Damase, Jacques, *Sonia Delaunay: Fashion And Fabrics,* Harry N. Abrams, Inc. Publishers, New York, 1991.

Droste, Magdalena, *Bauhaus, 1919-1933,* Benedikt Taschen Verlag GmbH, Köln, 1990.

Eliens, Titus M., Groot, Marjan, Leidelmeijer, Frans, eds., *Avant-Garde Design: Dutch Decorative Arts 1880-1940,* Philip Wilson, English language ed., London, 1997.

Farr, Michael, *Design In British Industry: A Mid-Century Survey,* University Press, Cambridge, 1955.

Goldfinger, Erno, *British Furniture Today,* Alec Tiranti Ltd, London, 1951.

Harrison, Charles, *English Art and Modernism: 1900-1939,* 2nd ed, Yale University Press, New Haven and London, 1994.

Hunt, Antony, *Textile Design,* Studio Publications, London and New York, new ed 1951.

Jackson, Lesley, *20th Century Pattern Design: Textile and Wallpaper Pioneers,* Mitchell Beazley, London, 2002.

Le Corbusier, *Towards A New Architecture,* trans. Frederick Etchells, Rodker, London, 1928.

Loos, Adolf, essay, 'Ornament And Crime', first published in English 1913, reprinted in A. Sarnitz, *Loos,* Taschen, Cologne, 2003.

MacCarthy, Fiona, *All Things Bright and Beautiful: Design in Britain 1830 to today,* George Allen and Unwin Ltd, London, 1972.

Maguire, Patrick and Woodham, Jonathan M, eds., *Design And Cultural Politics In Postwar Britain: the Britain Can Make It Exhibition of 1946,* Leicester University Press, London, 1997.

Marr, Andrew, *A History of Modern Britain,* Macmillan, London, 2007.

Morgan, Ann Lee, ed., *Contemporary Designers,* Macmillan Publishers Ltd, London, 1984.

Naylor, Colin, ed., *Contemporary Designers,* 2nd ed., St. James Press, Chicago and London, 1990.

Pascheles, Wolf, *Galerie der Sippurim,* Wolf Pascheles of Prague, 1847.

Pevsner, Nikolaus, *The Englishness of English Art,* Penguin Books ed., Harmondsworth, 1993.

Powell, Nicolas, *The Sacred Spring: The Arts In Vienna 1898-1918,* Studio Vista, London, 1974.

Prokop, Ursula, *Das Architekten und Designer – Ehepaar Jacques und Jacqueline Groag: Zwei vergessene Kunstler der Wiener Moderne,* Bohlau Verlag Wien-Köln-Weimar, 2005.

Reed, Christopher, *Bloomsbury Rooms: Modernism, Subculture, and Domesticity,* Yale University Press, New Haven and London, 2004.

Sparke, Penny, ed., *Did Britain Make It? : British Design in Context 1946-86,* The Design Council, London, 1986.

Strachey, Lytton, *Elizabeth and Essex: A Tragic History,* Penguin Books ed., Harmondsworth, 1950, reprinted 1985.

Stewart, Richard, *Design and British Industry,* John Murray Ltd, London, 1987.

Vergo, Peter, *Art in Vienna 1898-1918: Klimt, Kokoschka, Schiele and their Contemporaries,* Phaidon Press Limited, London, 1975.

Volker, Angela, *Textiles of the Wiener Werkstätte 1910-1932,* Thames and Hudson Ltd, London, 1994.

Woodham, Jonathan M., *Twentieth-Century Ornament,* Rizzoli International Publications Inc., New York, 1990.

Exhibition Catalogues and Related Publications

Black, Misha, *Architecture, Art and Design in Unison, A Tonic For the Nation: The Festival of Britain 1951,* ed. Mary Banham and Bevis Hillier, Thames and Hudson, 1976, p.83.

Blasting The Future: Vorticism in Britain 1910-1920, Jonathan Black et al., Philip Wilson Publishers, London, 2004.

Britain Can Make It: Exhibition Catalogue, The Council of Industrial Design, HMSO, London, 1946.

Britain Can Make It: Exhibition at the V&A Catalogue Supplement, The Council of Industrial Design, HMSO, London, 1946.

Chamberlain, R., Rayner, G., Stapleton, A., et al., *Austerity To Affluence: British Art And Design 1945-1962,* Merrell Holberton, London, 1997.

Design in the Festival: Illustrated Review Of British Goods, The Council of Industrial Design, HMSO, London, 1951.

Design '46: Survey of British Industrial Design as Displayed at the Britain Can Make It Exhibition, The Council of Industrial Design, HMSO, London, 1946.

Festival of Britain: 1951, Catalogue of Exhibits South Bank Exhibition, HMSO, London, 1951.

Festival of Britain: The South Bank Exhibition A Guide To The Story It Tells By Ian Cox, HMSO, London, 1951.

Harris, Jennifer, Lucienne Day: *A Career in Design,* The Whitworth Art Gallery, University of Manchester, 1993.

Historical and British Wallpapers, The Suffolk Galleries, organised by the Central Institute of Art and Design, The National Gallery, London, 1945.

Jackson, Lesley, *Robin and Lucienne Day: Pioneers of Contemporary Design,* Mitchell Beazley, London, 2001.

MacCarthy, Fiona and Nuttgens, Patrick, *Eye For Industry,* Lund Humphries Publishers Ltd, London, 1986.

McDowell, Colin, *Forties Fashion and The New Look,* Bloomsbury Publishing Plc, London, 1997.

Mendes, Valerie D. and Hinchcliffe, Frances M., *Ascher: Fabric Art Fashion,* The Victoria and Albert Museum, London, 1987.

Peat, Alan, *David Whitehead Ltd: Artist Designed Textiles 1952-1969,* Oldham Leisure Services, 1993.

Raoul Dufy 1877-1953, Brian Robertson and Sarah Wilson, eds., Arts Council of Great Britain, London, 1983.

Rayner, Geoffrey, Chamberlain, Richard, Stapleton, Annamarie, *Artists' Textiles in Britain 1945-1970: A Democratic Art,* Antique Collectors' Club, Old Martlesham, 2003.

Reconstruction: Designers in Britain 1945-1951, Target Gallery, London, 2001.

Schoeser, Mary, *Influential Europeans in British Craft and Design,* Crafts Council, London, 1992.

Seddon, Jill and Worden, Suzette, *Women Designing: Redefining Design in Britain between the Wars,* The University of Brighton, 1994.

Shone, Richard, et al., *The Art of Bloomsbury: Roger Fry, Vanessa Bell and Duncan Grant,* Tate Gallery Publishing Limited, London, 1999.

Utility Furniture And Fashion 1941-1951, Inner London Education Authority, 1974.

Vienna 1900: Vienna, Scotland And The European Avant-Garde, Peter Vergo et al., HMSO, London, 1983

Magazines and Periodicals

Ankwicz Von, Hans, 'Arbeiten von Hilde Blumberger – Wien', *Deutsche Kunst und Dekoration,* Vol. XXXIII, p. 125.

Art & Industry, Studio Publications, London and New York, 1936-1958.

Der Sonntag, Supplement of the newspaper *Der Wiener Tag,* 2nd August 1936.

Design For Industry, Studio Publications, London and New York, Jan-Dec 1959.

Design, The Council of Industrial Design, 1949-1973.

Designers in Britain, The Society of Industrial Artists, Alan Wingate, London, 1947-1954, André Deutsch, London, 1957-1965.

Furnishings From Britain, National Trade Press Ltd, London, 1948-1956.

House And Garden, Condé Nast Publications, London, 1949-1970.

New Home No 2, The Council of Industrial Design, HMSO, London, 1948.

Shaw, Mary, 'Buying For Your Home', *Furnishing Fabrics No 1,* The Council of Industrial Design, HMSO, London, 1946.

The Ambassador, The Ambassador Publishing Co, London, 1946-1968.

The Studio Year Book Of Decorative Art, Studio Publications, London and New York, 1943-1970.

The Textile Manufacturer, Joseph Appleby Ltd, Manchester, 1874-1975.

Index

Page numbers in bold type refer to illustrations and captions